Sweaty Mascots start Grease Fires

ANTON HAKOS

Tabby — this is the greatest $10 you'll ever read — Hell yeah GREG

Copyright © 2011 Anton Hakos

All rights reserved.

ISBN: 0615495915
ISBN-13: 978-0615495910

ABOUT THE BOOK

Names of people and places have been changed to protect the innocent. And the not so innocent. And me.

Find thought-provoking book club discussion questions at the end of the book.

1 INAUGURATION

"Ah, Shit!"

The heat from the grease fire struck me in the face and forced my head back and my eyes to squint. I stumbled backward. Determined, I forced my way back into the grill.

"Where are the hotdogs?" I screamed. I had just opened up the cover to our enormous cooking machine, but when I grabbed for what should have been a rack of hotdogs, there were no dogs to be found. I needed these dogs—the calls for food from the concession stands roared endlessly over the radio. I needed these dogs. I took a closer look and saw the dogs I needed, caged in their rack, at the bottom depths of the grill. I needed those dogs—burnt or not burnt. The thought of leaving them to burn to death never crossed my mind. I had to go in after them. But this was no normal grill. This baseball stadium's cooking machine was no prissy patio status symbol. No, this was far beyond backyard picnics. Our metallic beast cast a dark shadow over me and ran the length of a well-fancied 1960s American automobile. This was going to be no easy task.

With sweat dripping relentlessly into my already burning eyes, I lunged my body toward the whipping flames within the grill. The grill fought back with a tsunami-like wave of heat—heat so intense it was clearly visible to the naked eye. I fell backward from the blow, slipping on the grease-covered concrete below my feet. It took all the effort I had in my tired body not to fall to the ground. I sucked a breath, and with convincing determination, I once again lunged toward the grill, more aggressively than before. Flames crackled by my ears as my head entered the roar of the grill. For a moment, I thought of the life within this grill. I glanced at my boiling surroundings. Everything slowed for a moment. Twirling shapes of fire wickedly raced around the innards of the metal creature. An intense fear squeezed at my heart, but I mustered up enough courage to continue my mission. I drove my gloved hands into the bowels of the animal in search of lost hotdogs. It bit only once, snapping at my bare arms, causing a spastic twitch to quickly run up to my shoulder. Luckily, my determination carried me further, extending my arms near the hotdogs. The hairs on my arms fizzled away as my hands clamped onto the rack. Once attached, my arms quickly recoiled, pulling the dogs from the beast's mouth. My quick movement caused my foot to slip out from under me, sending me to the earth. I hung on to the dogs, however, and raised them up to look at my catch, revealing the most mangled, charred hotdogs ever witnessed. Ruined.

As I sulked over my destroyed hotdogs, the grill took its chance to fight back. The buildup of grease within the fiery grill caught ablaze and left me with flames spewing from the stainless steel gaps.

My counterpart Mel stood behind me, nervously shifting back and forth, aching to help, but I had acquired a firm individuality when problems arose at the grill that curbed my want for help—problems got solved much more quickly when I worked by myself. Therefore, I took most of the hits, burns, and bruises.

"Shit!"

"You want help, Hakos?" Mel asked sincerely in his positively thunderous, gospel-like voice.

"No, just keep racking, Mel!" I barked back at my only help.

"Okay," Mel agreed, turning around, continuing with the process of tearing open cases of frozen hotdogs and lining the dogs into the stainless steel racks.

I continued my battle with the furious grease fire. I jumped to the water hose, twisted the nozzle open and sprayed a pelting surge of water into the gargantuan grill. Yes, I knew water was not the suggested weapon in the case of a grease fire; however, a good constant blasting of water into the insides of this grill always dampened the monster out of commission. After several moments of my expert water attack on the fire, the flames vanished. This battle was mine. Unfortunately, this battle was one in a long lasting war with the massive grill we ultimately deemed "Hitler."

Hitler had me by the balls. I was a slave to this damnable beast. The beast was like any other wild animal in that it had a mouth and four feet—that is to say each corner of this beast was supported by a leg, and its opening measured wider than the jaws of a great white shark. We believed it to be more related to mystical dragons than any barbecuing phenomenon. Hitler possessed the ability to spit fire and regurgitate grilled food suitable for eating. Usually.

Damn this beast. This awful creature whose obstinacy knew how to bring my blood to a boil and send me home with a headache every night.

After momentarily taming the beast, I took a break and headed for the toilet. I walked the stairs that led from the grill to the bathroom. The cheap metal steps pinged like aluminum baseball bats under my feet. My body was slow and disgustingly warm. I looked up to the scoreboard, squinting through the heat in order to check the temperature. 104 degrees. I sighed and dragged my greased legs into the bathroom—the warm bathroom—its ecosystem consisted of a still, stale air, scented with a variety of pisses.

I hadn't sat on a toilet all day, and now, in the late innings of the game, my chance arrived. Covered with a film of grease and sweat, I pulled down my moist shorts and plopped on the sticky toilet—no reason to wipe it clean; the filth on my legs provided a sort of force field from infection. Shitting in these circumstances took a great Zen-like concentration. I kept my mind thinking beyond that of the heat that lazily strolled around my face, frequently caressing the sour sweat on my back and brow. Likewise, I avoided thinking about the fact that the grease caked on my body caused me to gain a few pounds. A break in concentration might lead me to puke. Instead, I thought about the happy moments in Southtown, starting from the earliest experiences.

The war between Hitler and me started at the beginning of my employment in minor league baseball. Ever since our introduction, our personalities clashed. Hitler refused to cooperate—he assured this through uneven cooking, frequent pilot light extinguishes and all out grease fires. Determined, I, on the other hand, fought desperately to make Hitler work, for without Hitler, thousands of baseball fans would go hungry. Why did I fight so ferociously to keep Hitler working? I cared little for the fans in the bleachers. I thought nothing of the team's revenue. Rather, I feared a massive ass chewing. My failure at the grill carried the possibility of losing an arm or my spleen. More specifically, I feared my boss more than I did any godly being. My team's general manager celebrated his ability to strike dominating fear into his employees. As a result, my sole mission on earth consisted of cooking thousands of hotdogs—only the grill Hitler stood in my way.

Allow me to back up... a couple of years earlier, I had graduated from college and was lacking any real direction. After considerable delay, I began sending resumes and applications all over the United States. I longed for the peculiar. I loathed the idea of working for the "traditional" business employer, overly obsessed with professionalism, dull suits and even duller ties. Thus, I found myself driving to Southtown from Akron, Ohio by way of a call from the Southtown local baseball team. Naïve and completely clueless, I packed my car with nothing more than my giddy smile. At twenty-three years old, I remained open to any opportunity. I knew little of frustration and negativity. My life to this point resembled a light-hearted movie about horses. With a passionate love for sports, I believed the baseball world might be the out-of-the-ordinary job I so eagerly wanted. So, I hopped in my car and drove in search of an unknown change, and, fuckin' hell, I got the change.

I whistled down the interstate, my hand out the window gliding on the breeze. I saw only smiles and love in my adventure—I knew of nothing that might bring down my sunny castle. I blasted the radio and enjoyed switching from station to station as I passed in and out of clear frequencies. Nothing could go wrong. Why would it? By some strange occurrence, a minor league baseball team, the Southtown Guitars, hired me to work in group sales, whatever that is. I honestly had no idea what "group sales" was. I imagined it as a circle of chairs in a lovely office room, where several young chaps like me brainstormed ideas about how to sell stuff. I would find this to be wrong.

Working in sports sounded quite attractive. Since I could remember, I lived for sports. I played football in the fall, baseball in the spring and basketball whenever I was bored with the other two. My hands constantly fidgeted with some ball, throwing it up and catching it on its way down; I was a sports fanatic. I knew all of the players' names, stats and positions—I specialized in Cleveland sports. I knew all the plays and what teams needed to work on what positions. I read the box scores in the paper everyday—as far as I was concerned, who needed the rest of the newspaper? I even invented my own leagues, keeping stats on an infinite number of players. My most elaborate league was my baseball league, where I collected all the known stats a boy could collect regarding baseball—BA, ERA, RBI; the lot of 'um. The Cleveland Cardinals led my baseball league, but the best part was that my friend ran the minor league counterpart to my major league, so teams in my league could call up my friend's minor league players. It was ridiculous. Nobody knew more about sports (especially Cleveland sports) than I did.

In family albums, my birthday pictures always included a cake with a Cleveland Browns helmet on it—aged 9, aged 10, aged 11, and so on. The most famous of course was my birthday in 1987. It was January, and the Browns were in the playoffs. There my friend, brother, and I sat, watching the Browns beat up on the Denver Broncos in the championship game. The winner of this game would go to the Super Bowl. We ate birthday cake and tacos, and we cheered, jumping up and down on the family room couches. The Browns were up by 10 with little time left. In a moment of spiritual realization, my friend spoke, "It doesn't make any sense. The Browns in the Super Bowl." We all smiled and jumped and screamed and...shit; in the end, they lost. The best birthday became the worst. We were all sick afterwards. We couldn't do anything. I think my friend just went home, dejected.

Back to the present, I shouted with joy as I crossed the Mason-Dixon. I never could have imagined what lay ahead...

My first Southern experience occurred in a McDonald's. Many say that these multinational corporations like McDonald's erase the diversity that exists in the world. There definitely exists some relevance to that; however, each McDonald's emits its own sense of multiculturalism.

At the time, I cared little for health. I walked into the southern McDonald's and ordered the traditional double-bubble-burger, fries, drink, and whatever the fuck else they sold. I needed a rest from driving. I parked myself in the corner of the restaurant and began ripping apart the paper that kept me from my juicy burger—good old burger, nothing better. Then, I saw it. I saw that the people sitting down looked very little like the people from Akron. These people wore auto-mechanic shirts and dirtied hats. They each spoke a tongue of nonsense and ate their fries while still chewing on tobacco. I thought little of this until I zoned in on the music being played through the sound system. What was this? What hideous sounds were these? This was a McDonald's? No such music played anywhere in the North. But, yes, the music I heard played, and the other creatures in the restaurant thought nothing of it, but I thought it strange. I looked at my burger to readjust myself. The burger tasted McDonaldese. And, later, after an earnest concentration, focused on the music, I realized Elvis' voice permeating through the sound system—"Ain't Nothing but a Hound Dog." The next twangy act permeating through the sound system sounded even less familiar. Boings, twangs and yodeling caused discomfort to my ear and jerked my nerves. My neck twitched to one side, revealing the awkward artwork on the Mickey D's walls—backwoods scenes of pre-industrial serenity. Turning to the parking lot, I realized that my car was the only car. Half-dilapidated American trucks of scarred rust surrounded my German auto.

2 THE JOB

Once I arrived in Southtown, I first needed to stop by the stadium to get the particulars about the job. I found the gated complex in a scrappy section of Southtown. I pulled through the gate and slowly drove my car up and over the hilly parking lot like a surfer navigating the waves of the ocean. While driving, the old stadium drew my eyes toward it. Built in the 1970s, the stadium's age showed—paint cracking and dulling, out of date lettering, foliage growing from gaps in the steel girders. I zoomed into the rolling parking lot. With each foot, the hilly parking lot tested my car's suspension. I stepped out of my car. The sun felt warm, but there was a moist chill in the air. I examined the old structure in closer detail. Facing the doors leading to the front office, I sensed that the stadium felt a bit uncomfortable, distorted and twisted. It sat in the ground a little so that I could actually look down into the concourse. The soily-white stands of the stadium blocked the view of the field from where I stood, but I could tell that I stood directly behind home plate. Brownish water damage spotted the stadium like a Dalmatian's coat, and the streams of unknown drainage flowed every-which-way from every-which direction. Peering up beyond the stands, I could see the scoreboard in the distance, and what a scoreboard it was—a gigantic guitar with the innings running up the neck of the guitar—so ridiculous and yet so great. I took a breath and walked through the front doors. I met Vera, the lady who called me about the job. She insisted I meet the general manager, Al, for a short interview. Wow—general manager—the title sounded so important. I would have settled for a captain. After a short wait of watching unknown people walking to and fro, Al waved me into his office. He asked me to sit down, and he sat opposite me behind his desk.

Al Barker looked at me and paused. Now, if the face staring back at me had been anyone else, it probably would have been described as a blank look. However, God never blessed Al with any face other than a scowl. Sure, Al might smile from time to time, but even his plastered scowl showed through his smiles. His laughs still scowled. His three-in-the-morning peaceful slumber face still scowled. Therefore, my first meeting with Al scared me to death. I forced a dumb smile on my face just to prove to Al my pleasant character—inside, my bowels rumbled with fear. During the pause, I took in my surroundings. Al wore a windbreaker and shorts, no socks, but loafers covered his feet. I gathered very little sense of style from him altogether, but his silver crew cut and a drill sergeant's face made him an easily drawable caricature. His office hinted disaster. Papers piled high. Promotional items crammed in every corner. A dried brown coffee mug smelled of rotten grounds. He removed a jacket from a chair but made no indication whether or not I was to sit there. I made an assumption and sat.

Finally, he spoke in a sort of short grunt, "You came all the way from Ohio, huh?"

"Yes," I quickly spoke so as to not give away how truly intimidated I felt.

"You like Southtown?"

"Yes."

"Oh, yeah?"

"Yeah."

The famous "oh, yeah?" comment. Al threw it out there more than anything. Mostly, he kept conversations down to a simple "Oh, yeah?" Looking back, the comment provided Al with a sort of time-out. The comment added nothing to the conversation; rather, it allowed Al to examine the situation. In this time, Al could study and analyze his prey. Or, maybe Al just didn't give a shit about the conversation. Sometimes though he spiced up the "oh, yeah" by changing the inflection—it meant nothing different; I think it merely allowed him some flexibility and entertainment.

"Shows some commitment driving all the way down here," he said. I agreed with a smile and a nod. "Now, I'm filled with the group sales positions right now, but I need some work in concessions."

Concessions? What the fuck's concessions? Without knowing, I shrugged and said, "Great."

"Oh, yeah? Great?" He said with a sly grin, while maintaining his scowl.

Is he fucking with me? I couldn't tell, but I decided that I shouldn't second-guess myself. I repeated, "Yeah, great."

He told me he could pay me no more than a thousand dollars a month. Again, I gave the "great" answer. He leaned back in his chair and turned his head toward the window behind him. He turned back to me and said, "BMW, huh?"—referring to my car. As a graduation gift from college, my parents went half way on a BMW 318i. Definitely a sweet car; however, people for the rest of my stay in Southtown would always razz me for it.

"Yeah."

"Fuckin' Beamer, huh?" he smirked. I know that my car usually signaled "spoiled brat" to most people, and I think Al questioned my ability to work in difficult conditions because of the car. He repeated several times that the job would be tough. People often questioned my capabilities. Knowing this, I quietly accepted each challenge.

The short interview ended with, "You got a place to stay down here?"

"I'm going to stay with my cousin who lives down here."

"Oh, yeah?" (I'm not really sure if a question mark is appropriate for the "oh yeah's." A question mark denotes some meaning to the phrase. However, I don't think the "oh yeah's" really deserve to be given status. So, from here on out, I'll quit with the question mark and just leave Al's quote with the more appropriate common period.)

"Yeah. Except, I haven't found him yet."

"Oh, yeah."

"Yeah, but I'll find him. I just have to call him."

Al smirked his lethargic smirk, we shook hands, and I left in my BMW.

3 MY COUSIN AND THE FIRST DAYS OF WORK

I found my cousin in no time. I ended up staying in his apartment for a couple of weeks until he found me a place of my own. He lived in a quaint area near the local college campus. I appreciated his generosity, and I hoped that we could get to know each other. A musician, he played at a couple of the local clubs and people knew him for it—this interested me. Unfortunately, I rarely saw him perform due to my baseball job—little did I know how consuming the baseball world would be.

We really only got to hang out once. The night before my first day at work, he invited me to a friend's house. His friend was an older, yet attractive, Greek woman who strove to get me drunk. Immediately, she introduced me to Ouzo by pouring me several shots in a row. She told me, "this is how the Greeks do it." She insisted that it was nothing and continued filling my glass. By the time we reached dinner I was seeing double. I sat to her left as she assumed the head of the table and led most of the conversation. I mainly listened—the company was much more informed and experienced on real life. I felt I had little to offer. The Greek woman kept filling my glass, and the conversations quickly changed from one to the next, gaining meaning and depth.

Then, the crowd got stuck talking about Mel Gibson in "Braveheart." Many at the table praised the movie's quality. But one vocal woman who sat across from me disagreed. In fact, she disagreed with a lot. She commented on everything. I perceived her to be obsessed with topping people's comments—she had always done just a little more and a little better than the previous person had. In this case, she claimed that, through reading a biography on William Wallace, she learned that he was actually a cruel man and not as learned as the movie made him out to be. As the night progressed, I began to dislike this lady and the characteristics she possessed. Her fascination with upsetting anyone's limelight sent shooting pains through my bowels—maybe it was the Ouzo.

By the end of the evening, I watched as the older crowd danced to traditional Greek music. Though running on Ouzo, I still felt intimidated by the pack of dancing revelers; therefore, I stood to the side, calling out genuine Greek cheers. The night faded into a blur of unfocused action.

Suddenly, my alarm rang—7 a.m. I needed to be at work by 8. I jumped into the shower, enjoying the gentle spray of warmth. In my morning haze, images of the night before ran through my mind. One image in particular caught my attention—the repeated scene of me downing shots of Ouzo. I paused a moment, felt my head, and realized I felt fine—no headache. I shrugged my shoulders and continued bathing.

I arrived at the stadium and sought out the only person I knew. I asked the receptionist where Vera might be, and she directed me to the corner room. There, I located my immediate superior and asked her about my job. She mentioned something to me about distributing team pocket schedules around the Southtown area. She introduced me to Aaron. Together, we were supposed to take cases of schedules and drive up and down the northeastern part of Southtown, stopping at every establishment, asking them if we could leave a pile of schedules. Seemed easy enough.

The entire day consisted of Aaron and me driving up to local businesses—mainly gas stations—saying, "Hello, we're with the Southtown Guitars. We're distributing schedules throughout the city, and we were hoping it'd be alright to leave a stack here by the register."

Our success rate hovered around fifty percent, but I quickly realized that distributing the schedules was not Aaron's real objective—making trades was. Aaron, who was relatively new at this game as well, had learned from some of the veterans that trades could be made. Some of the best trades came at food joints.

For instance, we drove up to an ice-cream place and began sweet-talking the girls behind the counter.

"Hi, we're with the Guitars," Aaron said.

"Oh, we love the Guitars," the girls replied with a thick Southern accent.

"Oh, really," he replied cunningly while peering over at me. "Well, we just happen to have these free passes to a game." The girls squealed. "Can we leave some schedules here by the register?"

"Oh, sure. Can we have some free passes?"

"Well, that depends," Aaron said with acute craftiness. "Can we get some ice cream?"

"What flavor do you want?"

The scheme was so simple. I stood in awe of the power of gifts. Over and over again we got free gifts by reaching into our pouch of endless free passes. I wanted to try the ploy.

We pulled up to a gas station, and I made a bet with Aaron that I could get a Playboy for free by trading some passes. I entered the station and asked the man if I could place some passes on the counter.

"No."

"I'm with the Guitars," I repeated.

"I know who you're with. I hate the Guitars and that damn owner they used to have."

"But we have a new owner."

"They all the same. It don't matter new or old."

"I have some free passes." I tried to bribe him. I didn't want to walk out carrying the schedules. I needed that Playboy. I refused to fail.

"I don't care if you've got a hundred free passes, son. I don't ever come out, and if I did come out, I'd come out on dollar night."

Being new, I knew nothing of dollar night. I searched for a response, but I had clearly lost. While I thought, he repeated, "Dollar night." He made a twisted gesture with his mouth and strangely stared me down. I left. I told Aaron about it, and we both laughed.

My first day on the job sent a sense of excitement through my body. I can get used to this. This is pretty cool.

I drove back to my cousin's apartment just a short distance away and I told him about my day. My dad, who was a bit skeptical of the job, called to see how things went, and I told him how well it went, spicing it up where ever I could in order to prove the job's greatness. I also told him about the Greek lady. We laughed a bit. My cousin and I watched baseball, ate dinner, and then I went to bed, excited for the next day.

I arrived at the stadium at 8 a.m., ready to saturate the Southtown community with Guitars schedules. I found Vera.

"I got a new job for you today." She started.

"Oh, okay," I was somewhat disappointed but looked forward to anything. I felt like a bundle of positive energy ready to accept any challenge.

"Now, I think I'm gonna have you re-organize the warehouse. Do you know where the warehouse is?"

"Not really." Actually, I had no fucking clue. I wondered why she thought I might know; I had only been there one day.

"No problem. I'll show you," she assured me. "Here's the job. The warehouse down there that stores all of our concessions supplies is a mess. I'm gonna fix that. You're gonna go down there and arrange it in some order... condiments, dry stuff, accessories... something. There's a guy already down there, but I don't trust him. I want you to take charge and clean my warehouse."

"Okay."

Together we walked the spiraling concourse to the warehouse. The walk took longer than it should have because of Vera's stiletto heels. I could never figure this out. We worked at a baseball stadium, but she insisted on wearing stiletto heels.

Vera showed me the warehouse, which was more of a shelter under the stadium stands—leaky roof, sticky floor, and a bunch of other questionable jazz sitting along with all the food supplies. Chips lined one wall all the way to the ceiling. Ketchup and mustard sat on the floor to the left. Straws and napkins sat in a puddle on the concrete. Plates and aluminum pans lay thrown from their cardboard cases, like the dead in a car bombing. With one look, I immediately saw demonic ghosts and lost souls swirling around the warehouse. I had to shake my head a bit before I made any sense of it all. What a job. Nostalgic memories of my messy basement as a kid kept me positive in this moment. I'll just have to do it, that's all. Then my helper popped up. His name: James.

James and I lacked any similarities. I was the spoiled naïve kid from the North, and James was the poor, skuzzy Southerner. He was goofy, and I was seriously inexperienced. Together we made a haphazard team, and I was the boss—me?

I began organizing the warehouse with immeasurable uncertainty. I scanned the muggy room and decided, "Ok, we'll put all the condiments in this corner, and that will leave us room to put the cups in this area."

"Alright," James responded with a fidgety nod of the head as he scanned the warehouse, "that'll work. That'll work real-good," he concluded his statement by clapping his hands together saying, "Dang, let's do it."

James' instant obedience to my suggestion boosted my confidence; however, I lacked experience in the outside world. Little did I know that cups came in three different sizes—16, 24, and 32 ounces. I just threw all the damn things together and believed it to be organized. Hell, the only organization experience I managed up to this point was my messy childhood basement, and, in that case, everything got thrown either in a closet, a drawer or under another piece of junk.

So, I went ahead with the directions, and James followed. During our work, a pick-up truck arrived, speeding down the concourse. I looked up, confused—never before had I seen a truck race through the concourse of any baseball game I attended in my life. My head tilted from the explosion of thoughts bouncing around my brain. What do I do when a racing pick-up truck is coming toward me? The truck skidded to a screeching halt, and some of the boxes sitting in the bed of the truck flew off onto the pavement. A very large man pulled himself from the driver's seat, lifted a box from the back, and walked over toward me. The man stood as high as a doorway. His belly resembled an enormous beach ball—perfectly round. His upper lip warmed by a mustache, the man looked with an intimidating scowl, similar to Al's, and a heated red face. The man marched over to us with the box. A Labrador retriever panted happily in the passenger seat of the truck.

"What the fuck are you doing?" he shouted, presenting me with my first taste of minor league abruptness—fuck this; fuck that; fuck it all—common office talk in baseball.

"We're orga..." The man interrupted. He dropped the box, and it landed with a clanging thud. The picture on the outside showed a metal shelving unit.

"You gotta put these fucking things together first." I later came to realize that "fuck" rivaled the word "the" in usefulness.

The large man continued, "Who's got you organizing the fucking storeroom?"

"Vera," I answered.

This reply caused the large man's face to contort in such a way that made me think a rock somehow got lodged between his ass cheeks. He shook his head and said, "You can't organize shit without putting these shelving units together. C'mon, get the rest of 'um."

James and I walked to the back of the truck and began unloading a series of shelving units. The large man stood on the back of the truck and handed down shelving unit after shelving unit to James and me. I imaged myself in Hell. Is Hell the unloading of an endless series of shelving units? I saw a long line of damned souls working as a conveyer belt, handing an infinite number of cases down the line—a line that never ended—the eternal line, working eternal hours, achieving eternal nothing. Little did I know, I would find myself unloading an endless series of many different objects throughout my stay in Southtown. Was it Hell?

"You guys have a fuckin' screwdriver?" the large man asked.

I kind of shook my head and looked at James to see if he knew the location of one. James kind of looked off in the distance, clueless to the fact a question had been asked. The large man shook his head with a disgusted grimace. "James," he said, "get me a fuckin' screwdriver from my office." At least now I knew the large man worked here.

James ran off, and the large man turned to me. "You new?" he blurted.

"Yes."

"Ahh, I don't think you're gonna need those, ahh, fuckin' khakis workin' out here." The previous day, khakis worked fine during schedule distribution.

"Yeah, I didn't know I was..." again, I did not finish my sentence.

"Fuck." the large man said as he looked into the warehouse. "What the fuck does she have you doin' in there?"

"We're organizing it." My response received a pissed-off head shaking by the large man—his trademark reaction to anything.

The large man started opening the box in front of him, and he began laying out the pieces. I tried to help as best I could, but I seemed to just get in the way.

"Where, ahh, ya from?" The phrase "ahh" made an appearance in almost every sentence the large man spoke.

"Akron, Ohio."

"Ohio? Fuck." He wiped an ever-growing puddle of sweat from his brow and continued, "I'm from Lima. You know where that is?"

I pretended to think for a moment and answered, "Nah, not really." He looked at me strangely, shook his head, and allowed a little arrogant burst of air from his nose that lifted his fat-jellied face.

James returned with the screwdriver, and the fat man showed us how to put one piece of the shelf together.

"You guys got it?" he asked.

"Yeah, sure." we both replied.

He looked into the warehouse and grimaced one last time, "The fuck." He squeezed back into the truck and peeled off down the concourse.

I turned to James, "Who was that?"

"Woofman."

"Woofman?"

"Yeah, he's like a dog trainer who's trained his dog to do acts on the field. It's pretty good."

I thought it strange that a dog trainer told us how to organize the warehouse, but I went along with building the shelves, which took hours. I scraped my hands to pieces and began swearing quite regularly. Soon enough, another employee came down to the warehouse.

"Hey, do you guys know if there are any cold plates down here?"

What the hell is a cold plate? Then I spoke, "I'm not sure. I didn't see any in there."

The guy walked into the warehouse, and I followed. He looked through some rummage, and then he turned and said, "Yeah, you're right. There's no cold plates down here." I felt pretty good about being right. "We need one for the picnic on Monday." He thought for a moment and then turned to me, "Hi, I'm Carson."

"Hello, I'm Hakos. Nice to meet you."

"So, you drove down from Akron to work here, eh?"

"Yup."

"I went to Bowling Green."

"Oh, yeah, I know it."

We chatted briefly, and then he asked with a snicker, "So, you've met The Woof."

"The woof?" I asked.

"The Woofman."

"Ah, yes. I guess I did."

"Piece of work, eh?" He said, still giggling.

"Yeah, I guess. I wasn't even sure who he was when he drove up and started barkin'."

"Ah, he's alright, just a little... well, let's just say he's Woofman. The Woof."

Our conversation continued. I asked him about baseball and the years he spent working in the business. I found out that he was Bill Carson, the assistant general manager, a highly debated title during my years with the Guitars.

I began to pick up on something while talking to Carson. I noticed that he joked about The Woofman and then turned around and said that the Woof was all right. I wondered if I made a mistake by going along with the joking. Did Carson try to trap me into disclosing what I thought? Did he try to get me to speak negatively of someone? Would he tell the general manager that I was talking bad of The Woof? I thought that next time I should just keep my big mouth shut. I wasn't my style anyhow. I never talked shit about someone who I thought was all right. In talking to Carson, I found it strange that he talked badly about someone he had just finished joking with minutes earlier. Such double talk didn't jibe with me early on. Baseball would eventually wake me up to the true world of devilish deceit and two-faced dragons. For the meantime, however, I remained in my world of romance and chivalry.

James failed to show up to work two days in a row, leaving me to handle the warehouse mess on my own. I took James home the first couple of days. He lived in a room in the bottom of some guy's house. James described his room as having a mildewed floor—always damp from the Southtown humidity. The room sounded disgusting, and I always wished for James to leave my car more quickly than he usually did. I always thought of James as being a somewhat sickly creature. The fact that he lived in a sickly room made him doubly sickly. I preferred he never show up again.

4 MEETING THE GRILL

I continued my work in the warehouse for the next couple of days. By this point, I mastered organization and all of the products. I felt quite comfortable with the job, and I enjoyed the atmosphere. I worked mostly on my own, accompanied only by the blaring music from the stadium sound system. The warm Southtown breeze lazily drifted about, slowing encircling my head. I sat on the ground mostly. Snags and stains already marred nearly every piece of clothing I owned in Southtown. It felt kind of nice,—ruining my clothes because my job called for it.

   This relaxation, however, came to a close by my fifth day on the job. The home opener. Still lacking any savvy or real-world realizations, I happily enjoyed all my duties, fixing shelving and moving cases of crap from here to there. But, alas, the day of the beast arrived on this fifth day. Game days, I would find, are a transformation from human life to super-human life. No. Scratch that. Not even a super hero could manage the confusion and nonsensicalities of a game day in minor league baseball. I believe only a supernatural entity could take on such a task and nonchalantly go about its daily life, only rarely experiencing flashback-causing hysteria. Because one would have to be dead in order not to feel the tension, fatigue, and stress that consumes a game day.

Sweaty Mascots start Grease Fires

So, there I was, fixing my hundredth shelving unit, when the enormous Woofman lurked up behind me.

"Hey, ahhh, we need you down at the grill...so, ahhh, clean that shit up and meet me down here around the corner."

"Okay." Again, I was in no shape psychologically to make any sense of his idiotic request. Therefore, I cleaned up my crap and followed the big bundle of a man around the corner.

I reached the so-called grill. It sat behind the 318 sign in right field. Just to the right of the grill rose a small structure about the size of a trailer home. This room contained a large pizza furnace, a cooler and freezer, and two deep sinks. To the left of the grill was another room, a trashed mess of stored items from years past. In front of the grill ascended a wall, blocking the crowd's view from what occurred behind it. Behind the grill, a grassy hill rose up about twenty feet. A rubber gas hose ran down the grassy hill from a large propane tank that linked to the grill at the bottom of the hill—a certain hazard for lawn mowers. Further down the home run fence toward centerfield, there sat a picnic area for groups to reserve. Many of the patrons who attended those picnic areas passed by the wall of the grill to get to their destination. The whole area looked more like a rundown neighborhood garage shop. It felt and smelled nothing like a kitchen. No grandma baked her cookies here. No mom spread her peanut butter and jelly sandwiches in this mess. It resembled nothing more than a trashed back alley in a trashed old city, lost of its industrial glory days. But all this mattered little to me at the time—this was my job.

The process for using the grill was a confusing operation. First, this grill contained a rotating system that used cage-like racks filled with hotdogs. Tables on one side supported the cages of cooked hotdogs, while tables on the other side held similar cages with raw dogs. Behind the tables sat a large steel machine that shot sporadic blasts of flames from its bowels. Later, I found out that the steel machine was the grill, Hitler.

Among all these hotdogs worked the Woof himself, coordinating a baffling cooking procedure. The procedure went as follows:

1. Take cases of hotdogs out of the freezer, which was located in a small shelter to the right.

2. Place the cases on the shelf situated under the "uncooked" table.

3. Open the cases and place the dogs in a cage-like rack.

4. Open the large door to the grill.

5. Place the rack of hotdogs on the rolling pins, which rotated from the front of the grill into some juice and then scrolled to the back of the grill, and then back to the front again (This process was to happen about three times for hotdogs and hamburgers, five to six times for chicken and pork chops).

6. When cooked, the rack is removed and placed on the "cooked" table, making sure that the same gloves that were used to place the raw material into the grill are not the same gloves used when removing the cooked.

7. Then, someone with "cooked" gloves takes the cooked food and dumps it into a cooler, similar to the type of cooler one would take on a picnic or to the beach.

8. Then, a runner took that cooler up to one of the seven concession stands on the concourse.

It seemed a simple process—simple, as long as everything ran smoothly.

Woofman explained the process to me and introduced me to Leo, who looked as though he were melting. Showers of sweat dripped from his brow down to his chin. From his white industrial strength dishwashing gloves, a mysterious brown liquid trickled. At Leo's feet there seemed to be an accumulation of all of his drippings. It all made for a fantastic Halloween costume. The entire area looked as though Leo spewed his funkiness all about—it was a disaster, but I could not image the work being too difficult. Woofman asked if I could handle it, and I told him I could. Then, he left to go play with his dog.

Once The Woof was gone, Leo embarked on a rampage of damnation. He cursed the fat Woof and shouted obscenities directed toward the general manager and anyone else in the office. Looking dreamy-eyed to the heavens, he devised a humorous tale that concluded with a violent end that went like this: "Al would be swearing up a storm, and I'd just take the gun and ace his brains across the office wall." I laughed, but I wondered why he was filled with so much rage.

Grilling was a difficult practice. We cooked for the entire stadium, and the demand was intense. The stadium held seven concession stands and several picnic areas that needed food from us. Up the stairs from the 318 sign sat stand six. From stand six, the concession stands circled in descending order around the stadium, ending with one, which lined up close to third base. Stand seven sat in the upper deck behind home plate. There were plenty of concession stands from which a hungry fan could choose, but the stands faced the parking lot, not the field. This meant a fan in line could not watch the game. This also meant that people became fidgety while waiting in line. Therefore, the concession stands needed to be speedy—stands could not wait on us for late arriving hot dogs if they ran out. Leo and I needed to make sure to stay one step ahead of the requests for more food.

In the beginning, Leo placed the racks onto the little pins that rolled around the extremely hot grill. However, after hours of scorching smoke streaming into his eyes, Leo surrendered to the pain, and I took over, starting a long relationship between the grill and me.

The gloves we used may have worked in allowing us to place frozen hotdogs into the racks, but the same gloves failed in protecting our hands from the 400-degree heat that festered within the innards of the grill. Frequently, the gloves tore from getting caught on some portion of the metal grill, placing one's skin in direct contact with the boiling racks.

It took no time at all for Leo and me to fall behind in the production of stadium meat. The customers were pillaging the concession stands of food. Therefore, the stand managers endlessly called for more food from us at the grill. We raced to keep up, but it was no use. In our hurry, we often lost track of who was racking and who was de-racking. Usually we didn't care. In this case, we often had uncooked gloves touching cooked food. Frozen blood crumbs from the raw chicken wings dropped onto cooked hamburgers, sizzling as they hit the rubbery skin. Frozen butterfly pork chops sat in brown juice from a mixture of cooked meats, flavoring the pork in the most interesting way. Everything happened so quickly, that most of this buffoonery didn't register with me at the time. It seemed the quickest method.

At one point, Leo said he had to leave to greet a client of his who had come out to the game and spent $4,000 dollars on a picnic. He ran back up into the stands, bitching. I turned and faced the grill. I could hear the flames inside fighting to get out. I squinted in pain with the thought that I was alone with the beast. I wanted to take a peek inside to see what it really was. It couldn't be that bad. It was just a grill. I slowly approached the grill, making sure not to slip in the discarded grease below. I placed my torn glove on the door handle to the front of the grill and began to lift the lid slowly. Immediately, a flash of heat whipped around my head, causing my entire face to clench. Then, without further hesitation, I threw open the lid. My sudden behavior upset the grill. In defiance, it spit a blazing round of grease onto my shirt. I counter-attacked by screaming and dropping the lid. But I refused to lose this battle. I charged toward the grill, threw open the lid, and peered inside despite the heat and flailing grease-spit. Inside festered a whirl of fire and heat. Unknown particles drifted around the grill's innards. I took them to be lost souls who had been snatched up by this wicked creature. A couple of moments were all I could take. I stepped back from the beast and let the lid drop. I was out of breath and scared, but I proved to the grill that I was willing to fight it.

While I was alone at the grill, I broke every possible health code. Hotdogs that fell on the ground usually found their way back into a rack. Lack of space caused cooked dogs to sit in uncooked chicken blood-juice momentarily while I attempted to open the flaming door to the grill with ripped gloves. I spent the entire experience with tearing, squinting eyes. Finally, the cooking produced a layer of grease on the concrete below, which made the ground slippery. Looking down at my shirt and pants, I could see only deep grease stains. I frantically tried to keep up with the demands for more hotdogs, but I fell short of keeping pace.

Soon enough, help came in the form of Mel Belle. While I frantically balanced the pain from the burns on my forearms and the panic surrounding my slothfulness, Mel joyfully strolled down the steps toward the grill. He praised the home opener with gleeful shouts and a glimmering smile. I looked up with my greased face.

"Who are you?" I asked painfully.

"Mel Belle. I'm the chef."

Awesome! "I'm Hakos. It's nice to have help."

With a smile on his face, Mel began inspecting the grill. "Oooh, this is a big one. You can cook all the food right here, can't ya?"

"Yeah," I answered.

Mel Belle was a large black man. He wore thick-lens glasses, a tight Guitars shirt that agonizingly stretched around his belly, and a Cubs hat. He was a jolly fellow who enjoyed praising the greatness of Jesus throughout the day. Only when told to do something did he escape from his heavenly self and begin seriously working. "Hey," I asked, "do you want to help me open these cases of dogs and place them in these racks?"

"Yeah." He began racking without gloves.

"Mel, put these gloves on while you rack the dogs."

He puckered his lips together and bobbed his head saying, "Yeah, okay. Gotta keep clean. Gotta be sanitizer, gotta be sanitizer."

"Cool. Thanks," I responded. I was thankful to have help, especially from a real chef. But something made me wonder about Mel. Whatever my feelings were, I gave him the benefit of the doubt and allowed him to start racking as I went to the bathroom. I needed a break—for the past couple of hours I saw nothing but hotdogs and felt nothing but stinging heat.

Standing at the urinal was bliss. I closed my eyes and took a deep breath as my urine streamed, warming my innards. I think a smile actually broke on my face, but it didn't last. My piss of paradise ended. I ran back to the grill and found Mel leaning against the fence cheering on the team.

"C'mon Guitars, c'mon!"

"Mel," I snapped, "aren't you cookin'?"

"Yeah, I got stuff on there."

"Is it done?"

"Probly, probly."

I rushed to the grill and opened up the lid. A blast of smoke hit me in the face, and I reacted with the usual clenched face. Half of the hamburgers were burned—burgers that needed to go up five minutes ago.

"Those are done," Mel declared.

"Shit!" I screamed. "Let's get those off! Maybe we can save some."

Mel reached over without gloves and grabbed the blazing metal rack. He managed to get the rack half off the pins before swinging his hands away. "Oooh, that's hot!"

"Shit, man! You gotta use gloves!" I turned to reach for some gloves to give him.

In the meantime, Mel tried again to grab the rack barehanded. He flung the rack into my elbow. With a hiss, a burst of steam raced from my arm. I screamed and ducked away. Somehow, Mel managed to get the rack to the table—the raw table of course.

"Sorry, Hakos. You okay?"

"Yeah, fine." I said through clenched teeth. "Just throw those burgers into the cooler and run them up to stand four."

Again, he puckered his lips and bobbed his head. I looked at my seared wound. It resembled some sort of Egyptian hieroglyphic. I could have seen an image of Mary in it, but the pain was too overwhelming. As Mel ran up with the few burgers that were still edible, I began inspecting the rest of the food in the grill. Soon enough, I heard a call on the walkie-talkie.

"Hakos, what's with these burgers?" It was Al. "They're burnt to hell." Al must have been in the concession stand when Mel delivered the food. Then I overheard Al say, "Mel, get back down there and do the cooking!"

My head dropped in the mass of smoke and I brushed my hands through my hair, moaning, "Fuck."

Later, I had the opportunity to run some hamburgs up to the concession stands. I ran a loaded cooler up the stairs to the concourse area. I rushed to stand three, wobbling back and forth from the weight of the cooler—the damn thing weighed a ton, but it was a sunny dream compared to the nightmares of the grill. I entered stand three and witnessed a complicated mix of order taking and food preparing. Employees rushed back and forth from the front of the stand to the back, yelling out orders to the people in the back who sloshed oozy cheese into paper containers filled with nachos. Workers' skin gleamed with layers of perspiration. Trashed containers and food littered the stand floor. Several floor fans blew warm hotdog air around the heads of the employees. Stand managers raced from one end to the other without any real sense. Maybe the grill was better, I thought. This stand was about a million degrees, and people kept bumping into each other.

Some faces looked stressed, others looked lost, still others lacked any expression at all.

"Those the dogs?" The stand manager asked.

I was still watching the chaotic process of the stand when the manager spoke to me. It took me a second to register her words. Finally, I responded, "They're hamburgs."

"We don't need hamburgers. We need dogs."

"Well, these are hamburgs."

"Well, take them somewhere else, cuz I got enough hamburgers." She opened up the warmer to reveal a drawer loaded with foil-wrapped hamburgers.

"Take 'um somewhere else?" I asked.

"I don't want them." She turned away and started filling nacho containers. I shrugged and walked to stand two.

"Whatcha got?" The manager of stand two shouted.

"Hamburgs."

"Well, where ya been? We're out. Set 'um here." He turned to a couple of employees, "Start bunning those burgers." The employees began filling hamburger buns with floppy hamburgers. Then they wrapped them into a foil. Finally, they stuffed the hamburgers into a warmer. The whole process confused me. As I stood watching, a disgusted look slowly swept across my face. I spaced out, entranced by the activities. After a few seconds of frozen shock, I shook myself from the daze and headed back to the grill for more fun.

Following four hours of continual hell, Woofman stomped back down to the grill and told us that we could stop cooking.

"Is the game over?" I asked, sweat caked across my face.

"Fuck no," Woofman said as he grabbed a hotdog from a cooler and ripped it in half with his mouth. "It's the eighth inning, and the stands are full of food. We don't want to waste too much. We'll let the shit dwindle down."

Sweaty Mascots start Grease Fires

"Okay," I responded. His speech made little sense to me, but I was happy to stop cooking.

"Al wants you to start cleaning this grill up. You can use the grease cleaner that's on the shelf in there."

"Clean the grill?" I asked.

"Clean everything. The floors. The tables. The grill. You gotta get up in the fucker n' spray it clean," he said this stooped over, pointing into the innards of the grill. Woofman grabbed another hotdog and walked off. Exhausted, I took a wiener from a rack and bit off a piece. Not too shabby.

By this point, Leo was back at the grill area, and together we began trying different meat products, reviewing the taste of each. Should it be cooked more? Less? Are the wings good? The burgers definitely suck. After critiquing the food, we started an hour-long process of cleaning the grill. This job seemed impossible. Guts of burgers and pork chops clung to the conveyer belt parts inside the grill. Muck and grime clung to the tables as well as the ground. During my hopeless scrubbing, I thought back to a time when some door-to-door salesman came to my mother's house. He was trying to sell this magic-like grease remover. My mom let the man in, and he showed how it wiped away years of filth from the oven. The shit actually worked, and I wished at this moment, while I scoured the insides of this enormous machine, that I had that magic formula. Together, Leo and I washed the grill area, making sure that the grill was spotless. At the same time, whatever we wiped off the grill, found its way permanently onto our clothes—they were ruined. It was midnight. Hitler and I had met, and Hitler had won.

Fuck. Were we finished? Not yet. During our cleaning of the grill, the other members of the staff cleaned the stadium. We had no cleaning crew; instead, the staff got together and picked up the trash. We trudged through row after row, picking up anything from a 16-ounce cup filled with tobacco chew to a half eaten hotdog smeared in nacho cheese. Sometimes, you would get lucky and find a used diaper. By the time Leo and I finished cleaning the grill, the staff was not quite finished cleaning the stands. So, I grabbed a trash bag and dragged my worn body through the rows.

This would be my life, day in and day out, for the next couple of baseball seasons. Why did I put up with this? I am not sure. I can only suggest that my youth blinded me to this exploitation. You would also think that I crawled through the stands in anguish. But I did not. Maybe it was the five soda pops I drank, or maybe it was the fact that I had been in constant motion for hours. Whatever it was, I leaped from row to row, shoveling gunk into my trash bag. I even had the energy to make jokes and laugh. Most of the other staff wore their clean staff shirts. By this point, I wore a torn t-shirt, stained with grease. Upon finishing with the trash pick-up, we were finally allowed to leave. One by one, we drove off, leaving the stadium for a few hours.

When I arrived at my cousin's, he was already asleep. I quietly made my way to my room, threw off my clothes, and dropped into bed. My preposterous energy ceded to a more rational exhaustion. I conked out without a second more spent. Not a moment later, the alarm rang. My arms struggled to lift my torso from the bed. Wincing, I swung my body around to a sitting position, but my feet could not touch the ground—it hurt to do so. I sat for a minute in a comatose state on the side of the bed. Eventually, I limped to the bathroom. I slowly washed and dried myself off even slower. Dark slime leisurely washed off my body and swirled down the drain. In time, I made it to my car and drove to work—my cousin still asleep. I felt horrible. With my eyes burning and my body throbbing, I felt like I had been run over and then backed over again by a tireless truck with rusted wheels.

When I arrived back at the stadium, I walked to the warehouse and began organizing the perpetual mess. As one-o'clock rolled around I heard a call on the walkie-talkie (we all had these walkies, which we called radios) that asked why nobody was cooking food yet. The voice was Al, and a blast of fear ran up and down my spine a couple times. I sat, frozen, waiting for my name to be called. I heard my name. I dropped what I was doing at the warehouse, and ran down to the grill. When I reached the grill, Al was holding a slushy box of thawed chicken. It was chicken from the previous night that I had never cooked—I had put it in the cooler.

"What's this shit?" Al asked me.

"Chicken."

"Why is it in the cooler?"

"I thought I should keep it cold over night."

"It goes in the fuckin' freezer. What the fuck." He got on his radio and told Vera that she had kids working at the grill who did not know the difference between a freezer and a cooler. He was right—I didn't. He threw the bag-o-chicken down and walked off, telling me to start the fucking grill.

The fear building inside me was incomparable to any other fear I had felt before in my life. I immediately concluded that upsetting Al was a bad idea. From here on out, I was under his spell. I turned to Mel, who I thought was a cook.

"Yeah, that's gotta go in the freeza. In the freeza," Mel said, shaking his head, "Al shouldn't talk like that. It ain't right."

I was disappointed in Chef Mel. I thought he should have told me about the difference between a cooler and a freezer earlier, but I kept my cool and realized that it was up to me from here on out to make all the decisions. That was the only way to make sure my ass would not get chewed.

"That's alright," I replied. "Let's get this grill lit."

"Yeah, okay, okay." Mel handed me the lighter, and I bent over at the side of the grill to light the pilot light.

The success rate of lighting the grill was comparable to the success rate of driving your car into a telephone pole while handling a samurai sword between your teeth and walking out without a scratch—success only happened by mistake. The whole process, unlike driving a car into a telephone pole, took Dalai Lama-like patience. One hand needed to be on the starter button, while the other one controlled the lighter. The slightest breeze (or breath for that matter) had the power to blow out the flame. Over and over again, I did this in a stooped position. And once one side of the grill was lit, I still had the other side to light. And when they were both lit, there was always the possibility that they might go out during the game. At times, I sat with my hand in the 500-degree grill, pressing on the starter button, just so we could cook something. It was a constant struggle.

Fortunately, it was only a five-day home stand, which was fine for me. I saw my cousin for the first time in a week, and I actually sat down once. I went back to organizing the warehouse during the off days. And soon after, I met who was to become my inseparable mentor.

5 BUTCH JOLLY

I had heard from Butch Jolly that his interview with Al turned into a shouting match. First, Butch waited for about an hour before Al accepted Butch into his office. While inside, Butch handed Al his resume. Al looked at the resume.

"You were in the military?"

"Yes, sir."

"Oh, yeah?"

Al looked back at the resume for a second. Then he laid it gently on the desk, turned it around so that it was readable to Butch, and slid it back to Butch.

"This doesn't mean shit to me." Whether Al was just being Al or he was in a bad mood is insignificant here. However, Butch, the Italian hothead that he was, took this gesture to be the greatest insult.

"What did you say?" Butch asked.

"I said that resume doesn't mean shit to me."

"Fuck you!" Butch shouted.

Al jumped from his seat and met Butch face to face over his desk. "You can't talk to me that way!" Al shouted back.

"I can talk to you any way I want!"

"Fuck you!"

They shouted with the entire office at a standstill, listening in amazement. Then, Butch burst from Al's office with his face beet-red. Soon after, Al casually walked out and said, "Get a load of that guy."

Al later called Butch and asked him if he wanted the job. Butch took the job (don't ask me why). Seems to make no sense, but Butch soon became a Guitar. He was hired to head the concessions department, the department that I was becoming more and more familiar with. When there were no games, I still drove around distributing schedules from time to time, but usually I stocked concession stands full of the essentials.

When I first met Butch, I had no idea who he was. I thought he was someone to replace the missing James. So, without any formal introduction, we began moving stuff from here to there, and we took food deliveries together. It was not until the second day of working together that I realized he was my boss.

I then asked him if Vera had hired him. He told me that Al had.

"Is Vera your boss?" I asked.

"Hell, no! I'm supposed to be taking over her job."

"Oh, so you're like my boss?" I was enlightened.

"I guess. I'm the Director of Concessions."

"Oh shit, I thought you were like me. You're my boss."

This revelation changed our relationship dramatically. I don't know if Butch felt differently, but I know I did. Some transformation occurred within my mind that made me take a more passive and subordinate role in our rapport. Maybe this is supposed to happen between directors and assistants—I don't know. But this single moment created a spark that continued to grow. An immense trust grew out of our bond, a kind of concrete trust I never felt before. We soon realized we could count on each other. We became a team, almost to the extent that we were an organization within the organization. Whatever it was, I followed Butch like a devoted dog, and he threw me the occasional treat. I followed the model that

Butch provided. His personality and actions would have a huge impact on my behavior.

Because of our job, Butch and I became inseparable. Without each other, we never would have finished our work. Sometimes, people called us by the other's name, but we knew our place. We shared the concessions office; it was really more of a place for derelicts, whoever was not heavily involved in sales became part of the concessions office. Woofman used the concessions office as his own—not sure why he needed an office, but apparently he did, and his massiveness took up a lot of space. Butch and I made our calls to the different food vendors from this office. We placed orders for popcorn, hotdogs, soda, beer, restaurant supplies, ice cream, and anything else that went into running a concessions department. We wore ball caps and shorts, and we usually looked grimy as all hell. Butch kept most of the important stuff on his desk. My desk collected a random mix of cluttered stories and nonsensical pictures—stuff I did in my limited spare time. My doodles and stories got me strange looks and labeled a goof, but they were one way to keep my sanity in my new environment. I tried to lighten the mood, making people laugh. One of the papers posted at my desk was my list of "People to Blow Up," which included a series of condemnations against the group sales department.

I enjoyed the concessions office, hell it was air-conditioned. Mostly, Butch and I strenuously labored outside under the blazing rays of the Southern sun. We unloaded case upon case of food from delivery trucks. We lacked the blessings of a pallet-jack or forklift; instead, we unloaded everything piece by piece with our arms and backs. Butch stood in the delivery truck, tossing cases of product down to me. I stood in the bed of our all-purpose blue pick-up truck, our concessions transport vehicle. As I loaded the items into the bed, I made sure to carefully balance everything so that all the pieces would survive the winding drive to the warehouse. We did the cold and frozen items first in order to keep them fresh; however, after sitting on the truck for a while, the cardboard cases slowly deteriorated. Usually, by the time we reached the freezer, the cases were like formless mush. However, we spent hours rotating our food and beverage supply in order to ensure freshness.

We lugged cumbersome kegs around the different concession stands, jamming the kegs into coolers, piling them on top of each other, while inhaling and slipping on stale beer. We always wondered who would be the first to drop a keg on their foot.

We programmed registers and unclogged drains. We painted and cleaned, forever it seemed. We rarely took breaks, but all the while we worked together, forming an indivisible team.

We even tricked Buck Moss, the most devoted Guitars fan who came to every game hours before the first pitch and sat in his favorite seat, high above home plate in the upper seating section, allowing him to cheer on the staff as they struggled to set up for the game. Buck Moss yelled all sorts of phrases down to us. "Good job, Butch" and "That'a boy, Butch" were some of his usual sayings. But these sayings were used even if it was me running about. Buck Moss did not differentiate between us—so I was always Butch. Sometimes, Buck Moss could be caught roaming the concourse area. He was a man of about fifty years with a big blob of a belly that would have rolled over his pants if he had not jacked his pants up so high. The famous belt buckle held everything in place. Buck Moss often asked people to "touch the buckle" as he walked toward you. You may have guessed by now that Buck Moss was not really up to par mentally—you're right! If asked too many questions, Buck Moss would stare somewhat to the side and reply with a one-word monotone answer. But usually, he spoke with a kind of squeal. He walked slowly with very little mobility, in little sliding steps. He gripped a cane, which he did not use, and he kind of just scooted along in his black sneakers. Buck Moss' buddy, Gary, was a young boy who brought a bucket of rubber bands to every game and sat next to Buck Moss. I never figured it out.

Anyway, Buck Moss often squealed down to Butch and me, "I see you, Butch. I see you."

Butch and I would just laugh and say rude comments back to Buck Moss under our breath or to each other. Nobody ever really wanted to hurt Buck Moss—he was just a man with a mental disability who didn't really mean any harm; though, he could be quite scary to an ignorant kid such as myself.

One time, Buck Moss insisted on screaming down at Butch, while we were down on the field, "I see you, Butch. I see you."

Butch finally got fed up and screamed back up at Buck Moss, "Go fuck yourself Buck!"

Buck Moss sat speechless and his head turned to the side. A nervous smile appeared on his face.

"You hear me, Buck? Go fuck yourself!"

All of a sudden, Buck Moss snapped. He became enraged, and he shouted damnations upon us all, "You can't talk to me that way! You're gonna go to hell! You can't say that to me!" Butch spoke with such hellfire and brimstone as to suggest that the Rapture had exploded within the crumbling walls of the Guitars Stadium.

Butch continued as the rest of us listened in awe, "Fuck you! Fuck you! Fuck you, Buck!"

Usually, Buck Moss emitted a joyous air. Independently he was a quiet man who went about his business. This day was different as he shouted his calls for redemption. After watching such agitation amplified in such a matter, I believed Buck Moss to have lost his mind, more so than he had already. Would he return? Was this the end of hearing Buck Moss spur us workers on from his throne above? I wondered if Buck Moss had been scarred beyond repair. But the next day, Buck Moss returned and sat in his same seat with his cane and shouted down to all of us with positive encouragement, "You get 'um, Butch. Butch? Butch?"

"What Buck?" Butch reluctantly asked.
"Guitars gonna win today, Butch?"
"No."
"Why not?"
"Cuz they suck your momma's tit, Buck."
"No they don't?"
"Yes they do, Buck. Have you ever sucked your momma's tit, Buck?"
"No."
"Haven't you seen every game, Buck?"
"No."
"Yes you have, ya fuck."
"No."
"Buck?"
No answer.
"Buck?"

No answer. Again, Butch had upset Buck. And again, Buck came back the next game cheerier than a nerd-kid who accidentally walks in on his geeky friend's hot naked sister.

We didn't harass Buck Moss because we didn't like him. We did it because we needed something to keep our minds off of our long hard days. Like my cartoons in the office, making fun of Buck Moss gave us an outlet to laugh at.

6 THE RODRIGUEZ BROTHERS

Supposedly, the Rodriguez brothers made their way to Southtown by breaching the same border many immigrants cross when passing from Mexico to the United States. They risked their lives to work good paying jobs in America. Back home, the Rodriguez brothers picked strawberries for very little money, but each summer they escaped the low wages of Mexico and ventured into the wealth of America. Through the inhospitable desert climate to border guards with guns, the Rodriguez brothers overcame it all in order to play the role of stadium custodians.

Similar to their committed efforts to entering the United States, the Rodriguez brothers worked with a tireless drive. A permanent gleam of sweat wrapped their heads like halos. Their job consisted of the following:

1. Clean everything, including the stadium bleachers and other seating, the sky boxes, the bathrooms, the concourse.
2. Stuff 1,000 goody bags (favors taken home by the fans after the game) full of promotional incentives.
3. Live in the storage room on the third floor.
4. Try to communicate through the language barrier.

The Rodriguez brothers spoke virtually no English, and most of the Guitars staff spoke absolutely no Spanish, except for perhaps some dirty words taught to us by the Rodriguez brothers.

Though the Rodriguez brothers specialized in janitorial work, this did not make them the bottom of the totem pole. In fact, they made nearly three times my wages when I started (I know this because one afternoon they caught sight of my check and laughed. I took a look at theirs and could not believe my eyes). Not only did they surpass me in wealth, but they also surpassed me in rank. The Rodriguez brothers possessed some ceremonial rank of great respect. Merely being a Rodriguez guaranteed you some level of respect. Not to mention, I often found myself slaving over many of the same jobs as the Rodriguez brothers.

One afternoon, while the Rodriguez brothers finished cooking some traditional Mexican pollo dish up in the restaurant, Carson walked in and began speaking to the brothers. Carson was the only employee who spoke Spanish fluently—he was the translator. I stuffed down some unknown Mexican food and watched as they spoke. They finished speaking and Carson told me that I could help the Rodriguez brothers with stuffing goody bags. I was thrilled.

In the press box, we sat in an assembly line around a table full of promotional fliers. We passed the bags from one to the other, stuffing two to three papers at a time. The Rodriguez brothers talked. I listened, occasionally trying to say something—this usually wound up in some hilarious laughing fit by the Rodriguez brothers. The bags rotated around the table, and we listened to festive Mexican music.

On one occasion, I brought in the band The Gypsy Kings, thinking this Spanish flare might get me in good with the Rodriguez brothers. They grimaced upon hearing it and shook their heads. How was I to know that The Gypsy Kings were French? Again, they laughed at me. So, here I was, the lowest of the low at the Guitars, a grill boy who even looked up to the illegal custodial Mexicans.

Other times I found myself cleaning the stadium alongside the Rodriguez Brothers. We cleaned the stadium by blasting it with enormous fire hoses. The Rodriguez Brothers always took the lead; I followed dragging the hose behind so that it wouldn't get caught on a corner.

"Vamanos! Vamanos!" the Rodriguez Brothers yelled, passionately encouraging me to keep up with their flooding of the stands.

The torment of the fire hoses blew everything to a central location where we could more easily sweep up the trash. I don't know how much water this wasted, but it was quite effective. Not to mention, it allowed us to cool off some in the Southtown heat.

When I finished assisting the Rodriguez Brothers, I was back to my concession duties.

"Hasta mañana, cabrón," they'd say.

PART II

7 GETTIN' MY FEET WET

My first season with the Guitars developed into a tiring adventure in the working world. Though my job consisted of dirt, grime, extensive muscle work, sweat, fatigue, varying degrees of irrationality by the staff, an uncooperative grill, and no time to myself, my upbeat, wide-eyed, youthful self allowed me to keep pushing—naivety can be so great. I possessed an endless amount of positive energy. I enjoyed all the characteristics needed for my job. I gladly accepted the physical demands. This was just an extension of school recess. Any misery that presented itself quickly vanished due to my energetic personality.

As soon as Al hired Butch, Butch and Vera bashed heads on what should be done with the concession department. Quite frankly, Vera lacked the skills needed for human interaction let alone the skills needed for concessions. Soon enough, after constant bickering, Al canned Vera, which allowed Butch and me free reign in the concessions department; however, this also forced Al to throw more crap Butch's way.

Al watched his staff closely. Perhaps his face was not always peering over your shoulder, but he did not need to play the role of shadow. Al had brains and influence—he used these to gain knowledge about the happenings around his stadium. Similar to Soviet eyes and ears, Al used his employees, very tactfully, against each other. Al knew that people liked to talk; therefore, Al simply got people talking enough so that he could gain information about his team. Al's sidekick Carson poked around, gathering information. We all knew this, and we all had to be on our constant guard. We developed secret codes for over the radio—everything from "Can you check the cooler in the kitchen for more dogs" to "We're fucked; get down to the grill in a hurry." Butch and I revolved our codes around the Philadelphia Flyers. "The Flyers are losing" meant the latter message.

In time, the groundskeeper quit, and Butch and I became the grounds crew. We now had to take deliveries, stock stands, maintain an inventory, cook the food, deliver the food, mow and water the field, and many other insanities. The abundance of work forced us to come in at 6 a.m. and (on a game day) leave around 1 a.m. The only salvation we found at work comprised of setting up beds under our desks. It was actually quite comfortable.

Butch and I took to drinking ourselves to calm at Butch's house. Usually, Butch reminisced about some youthful day when he and his friends "were gettin' all fucked up." The stories always made me laugh, and I often wondered how he never killed himself. Other times, he told me of some experiences in the army—these never really interested me. I typically sat back, listened and enjoyed our friendship. If we did not seek shelter at Butch's place, sometimes we looked for fun around the stadium. We could always hide out in a concession stand and drink some beer. The restaurant attached to the stadium, which sat high above home plate, provided adequate food for us to feast on. Other times we found adventure just outside the stadium. Such as the time a concession stand manager asked us if we were looking for a good time.

"Hakos?" he asked.

"Yeah?"

Sweaty Mascots start Grease Fires

"You like pussy?"

"Sure." My response was not too confident. The question took me off guard.

"I got some pussy."

"Huh?"

"I know some girls who'll suck your dick."

"Oh, yeah?"

"You like your dick sucked?"

"Sure. Why not?"

"Butch said he was comin' by my place tonight. It's right down the road here." He motioned his hand toward the outside of the stadium. "Butch knows where to go. You should come too."

"Ok."

"You like pussy?"

"Yeah."

He smiled and pointed at me, "You won't be disappointed."

Later, Butch caught up to me and asked me if I had been asked to get pussy.

"Fuck. I'm not too sure about this," Butch said while laughing. "But I think I'm gonna go. Are you?"

"Yeah, sure."

After the game, I followed Butch out to this guy's house. It was about two blocks from the stadium—not the best area in town.

"There he is," Butch said and pointed at the stand manager.

"Hey, boys, you ready for some pussy?"

Butch and I looked at each other and laughed.

"Sure," We both said.

The guy offered us some beer. We kind of mingled for a while. The guy told us of a time when he got drunk and trashed some party. Butch presented one of his stories about getting all fucked up. After a while, the pussy showed up.

"There she is," the guy said.

In the distance was a short woman who walked toward us.

"She may be short, but she can suck a good dick," the guy said, and we all laughed. "Of course, then what dick sucker ain't good?" We laughed harder.

I squinted and tried to make out the woman. Suddenly, the moonlight shined on her just right. My eyes flashed wider. She was a midget—an ugly midget. Now, I have nothing against midgets, but I was expecting a tall super model by the way the guy was promoting his pussy connections.

"I gotta get going," I said. Quite honestly, I showed up just for the fun of it all and to get a good laugh. I certainly never considered getting my dick sucked no matter the girl. Sleeping around with just anyone was never my cup of tea. Showing up to a guy's house to have my dick sucked by an unknown midget was definitely not one of my sexual fantasies. The moment felt too uncomfortable, and I felt the fun melting away. The fact that the neighborhood was not the greatest did not help either.

"What? You ain't staying?" the guy asked. Butch looked at me with a smile.

"Nah. I'm leaving. Bye." Butch and I waved our goodbyes.

"You missin' out on some fine pussy."

When I got into work the next day, Butch told me that the midget sucked his dick. He sat on the stairs leading up to this guy's house, and the midget just walked up to his cock and sucked it good and hard.

"What?" I was laughing my ass off.

"Hey. What difference does it make? I got my dick sucked." Butch seemed to believe this strange logic. I was not quite ready to buy it.

8 RADIO 40 AND THE COOKING FIASCO

I carried radio 40. Everyone knew this. A board posted on the wall in the office told who used what radio. Every night we placed our radio in the matching slot for charging. During one night at the grill, I made a move for my radio to call Butch about some hotdogs. My radio wasn't there. Where was it? I always kept my radio hooked to my grease-stained pants. Since I was in a hurry, I asked Mel for his, and he flipped me his radio. I called Butch about the dogs. After talking, I turned my head to look for my radio, and it was nowhere to be found. Then, I did one of those "Oh yeah, I know where I put it" things, but it wasn't there either. I decided to worry about the radio later. There were more pressing needs—cooking.

Butch and I were both new to the concessions business, and we didn't always get things exactly right. Sometimes, we didn't even get close to right. On this day, the last day of the home stand, the crowd poured into the stadium in unexpectedly high numbers. Prior to the game, Butch feared over-ordering from our food distributor. There was always the dread of being left with some cumbersome inventory. Therefore, on this particular day, Butch decided to roll the dice and not call for any extra hotdogs on the last order. Instead, he wanted to let our stock of dogs run out. We worked the numbers before the game, and we both thought we had enough.

The immense crowd was a hungry on that day. These humans who stormed into the stadium seemed to have starved themselves over a month's period of time. These beastly people flocked into the stadium like vultures—they never let the concession stands out of their sight. The lines reached astronomical lengths. This only made the situation worse—people order more when the lines are longer to prevent an extra trip. People ordered five to ten hotdogs at a time at the concession stands. To make things worse, the picnics (which were booked) ate everything in sight as well. It was pure madness. Civilization did not exist here. People reverted to their prehistoric selves. Hunched and grunting, these fans of ours romped around the concourse in search of any loose food. I could barely look—it was too awful. Upon realizing that we were running out of hotdogs in the third inning, I emergency-called Butch with the code, "The Flyers are losing." Butch rushed down to the grill, and I told him that we were fucked.

"You gotta ration what's left! Only send shit up if it is perfectly necessary," he said and then added, "I'll go order more dogs." He ran off, and I sat wondering how he was going to get more dogs to the stadium on time, especially on a Sunday.

Butch needed to call the president of our distributor (who we knew well) and sweet-talk him into delivering on a day when there were no deliveries. Once Butch hung up the phone, the president needed to jump in his Lincoln, race to the warehouse and stuff his car full of cases of hotdogs. Then, he needed to drive to the stadium so that I could grill them. My nerves tried to take hold, and I tried to shake them off.

I listened to Butch's advice and sent up just a few dogs at a time when a concession stand or picnic called for more. If a staff member called for 100 more dogs to a picnic, I sent 50. After a while though, I began sending 25 or 15. The numbers of dogs I sent kept getting smaller, and the calls from the picnics kept getting larger. There was another problem. Before each game, I calculated how many dogs each stand and picnic would need. Something was peculiar about one of the picnics that night. The numbers of hotdogs the picnic asked for was not adding up to the number that I had written down earlier in the day. The group sales person told me that the picnic paid for 150 people. Even though it was an all-you-can-eat picnic, I thought it strange that the sales person who was calling for more dogs had already called for 500 dogs. It was this insanity that really hurt our food production.

The fact that Butch disappeared for a half an hour and no dogs appeared left my mind. I became obsessed with the fact that someone gave me phony numbers on a picnic, and the calls for more food kept coming. The stress ate at my patience and ability to concentrate.

"Hakos, we need 150 more dogs," the radio cried.

"Okay," I answered.

"Now!" The salesman on the other side lost his patience with my sending scraps. He snapped at me, and this caused a sort of fire comparable to that of the grill to spark inside of me. Then he came back with, "This is bullshit!"

Then, what I most feared happened. Al got on the radio, "Butch, where the fuck are those dogs?"

Butch failed to answer because he was on the phone ordering hotdogs.

"Hakos," Al barked, "everything okay down there?"

In mid-rack, I scooped up Mel's radio with one hand and blurted, "Yes." Then, I tossed the radio across the table, causing it to fall to the ground. The radio screamed with a painful "beep!"

"Then, where are those dogs?" the salesman shouted.

I refused to answer any more questions. I threw two hotdogs into a cooler and told one of my runners to take the cooler over to the picnic. The young kid smirked, picked up the cooler, and ran across the stadium to the other side where the picnic was being held.

"Where are those dogs, Hakos?" shouted the salesman.

"Hakos?" Al screamed.

I picked up the radio and answered, "I just sent some. They should be there in a second."

Just then, Butch came down. "How's it going?"

"Shit. I just sent a cooler with two dogs to the picnic." I grinned, unable to laugh because of the tension in the air. Butch, on the other hand, laughed hard, impressed with my rebellious action.

Just then, Butch looked passed my shoulder. "We got dogs coming."

A car, packed with cases of dogs, sped up to the grill. A man in a suit stepped out of the car and spoke in a pleasant Southern accent, "Hey, Butch, I gotch yer dogs."

Quickly, the runners and I rushed to the car and grabbed as many cases as we could. Mel began splitting open the cases, racking them with blundered perfection. It was a beautiful moment. With the radio still shouting for more dogs, my stomach eased, knowing that in 15 minutes, we would have cooked hotdogs.

After the excitement of the hotdog arrival, I asked Butch how he got the owner to come out on a Sunday with dogs.

"Cuz I'm long dick daddy from Cincinnati." Every once in a while, Butch uttered some comically arrogant remark. His self-confidence was his strength, and it seemed to help him prevail in any sticky situation.

Eventually, in order to suffice the calls for more dogs, we sent shit loads of dogs to the picnics. The picnics and the concession stands were full. Sometimes I took a cooler loaded with dogs up to the stands. I raced up the stairs to the concourse lugging pounds of hotdogs, destroying my back with every step. I turned the corner and saw one of our interns drop a foil pan of chunked, brown grease splat on the ground. He looked up and saw me and ran off into the closest concession stand. I continued carrying my weight, assuming the kid was going to clean his mess. Later, when I returned back the Hitler, I noticed the spill

Sweaty Mascots start Grease Fires

of grease still glistening in the Southtown sun. I ran back to finish my duties at the grill. Later, I got bitched out for letting the grease sit. When asked about the mess, the intern replied, "At first, when I dropped it, it was my responsibility; but when Hakos saw it, it became his responsibility."

This kid, Stan, stayed with me in my apartment for a while, until he could find a suitable place. I told him, "Just a few days," but he never left. He was studying to be a lawyer, and he thought of himself above the rest of us. He spent most of his time working with groups and picnics and somehow got out of the real horrific work. When my landlord found out that I let some guy stay with me, I got tossed. Stan saw nothing wrong with this and immediately moved in with this girlfriend. I on the other hand, struggled for the next few days with finding a place to stay—not what I wanted to do during the season.

Stan worked a lot with the group sales guys. I'm not sure if Stan was an idiot, or if he merely refused to follow our unspoken rule of "Don't Rat." Whatever the case, Stan worked the picnic that was calling me out over the radio. Later, he and the head group sales guy stopped by the grill. Knowing that pissing me (the producer of all food at the stadium) off was a bad thing, the salesman who blatantly called me out over the radio decided to sweet talk me. He apologized for what he did, but by this point, I realized that he was a salesman, and he was selling me his story. Stan nodded in agreement, as if I cared for his opinion at this point. I sold the salesman instead by pretending to give a shit. My innocence was slipping away. I could only think through a filter of anger.

"I was trying to cook the shit as fast as I could," I said.

"I understand that. But you have to understand that I had people standing there in line waiting for food. These people paid big bucks."

"I realize that, but I don't want to over produce. It's the last game of the home stand, and the picnic sheet said only 100 or so people."

"Hey, they just kept eating."

I knew this to be bullshit. I knew that he had sold the picnic at a cheaper price just to get the business to book a picnic. Then, he pretended that only 100 were going to show. This is where he got fucked though. He forgot about the grill factor. I turned to the coolers of leftover hotdogs, and showed the salesman what happened since he kept calling for 100 and 200 dogs at a time. He turned and saw five coolers full of steaming hotdogs. Once the Hotdog Savior arrived with the cases of dogs, Butch told me to just start cooking everything. So, I just kept cooking, leaving me with about 3,000 left over dogs. The fucker laughed and then turned to the field with the evening breeze rushing over his baldhead.

"Hakos, I don't have the answers. But what happened today was bullshit." He said it in a sort of thought provoking, philosophical tone. I just wanted to kick his ass. But I refused to burn any bridges. Being everybody's friend was the way to go. The last thing I wanted was someone going behind my back—a growing trend in the office.

With the end of the game, came the traditional cleaning of the grill. Butch came down to see how we were doing, and I showed him the leftovers.

"What should we do with these?" I asked.

Mel decided to give his two cents, "Can't save those," he said with his puckered lips. "Too many. Just gotta throw those away. Can't save 'um."

Butch thought for a moment, and then replied, "Fuck...keep 'um. Throw 'um in the freezer. We'll use 'um for the next home stand."

"Okay," I responded in my usual obedient tone.

Mel bobbed his head in agreement. "They be okay. They be okay."

"Wait. When is the next home stand?" Butch asked.

"Eight days," I replied.

This caused more to pour out of Mel's mouth, "Too long. Gotta throw those out. They'll get nasty."

"Fuck it. Keep 'um," Butch insisted.

"That's all you can do. Gotta keep 'um," Mel agreed.

So, Mel and I lugged loaded coolers of freshly cooked dogs into the freezer. I had not seen what cooked hotdogs looked like after sitting in the freezer. But I did know what they looked like after a night in the cooler. For whatever reason, refrigerator-kept hotdogs produce some gelatinous material overnight. The day-old refrigerated dogs were often still warm, and they jiggled in their jelly. I wondered if it was safe to merely throw the dogs back into the grill to reheat them, but I never questioned the decision to do so. Would the freezer produce something different? Would the dogs last for eight days in the freezer? These were questions I had, but, after this night, I couldn't have cared less. Mel and I finished stacking the coolers on top of one another in the freezer, I pressed the freezer door closed and preceded to clean up the stands. The home stand was over, and I was thrilled.

9 RADIO 40 STILL LOST AND THE EMPLOYEES WON'T HELP ME LOOK FOR IT

I made one last scan for my radio 40, looking in coolers around the stadium, but the damn thing was not to be found. I tried to keep it a secret, but secrets were hard to come by in this environment. People laughed at how the loss of the radio was going to come out of my paycheck. I pretended to laugh, but I feared what my carelessness might bring upon my head. Though the staff convinced me that I lost the noise-emitting piece of shit, I knew someone took it from me and was playing a game. Why would someone steal it? The answer would reveal itself in time, but not this night.

In those early days, Butch didn't have a car. This meant that I picked up Butch in the morning and drove him home at night. We started a nightly ritual of picking up a tallboy beer at the gas station and drinking it on his back porch. After an 18-hour day of constant muscle power, one tallboy really messed me up. In fact, the first time we did this was the first time I ever drove with a buzz. Driving my car home without the ability to completely focus scared the shit out of me at first but settled in as the norm after a while. There's a bizarre sensation of being in

Sweaty Mascots start Grease Fires

that warped state between sobriety and drunkenness. The relaxing swirling in my head that restricted my traffic attentiveness complimented the warm, late-night drives home.

On Butch's porch, he told stories of his younger days—drinking, getting wasted, taking drugs, all that sort of shit. I enjoyed listening to most of his stories, but usually I had to stop him short of finishing them all in one night. By the end of my association with Butch, I think I heard all of his stories at least four times, but they were funny nonetheless.

Butch told one story about when he visited a friend at college. It was a frigid weekend in southern Ohio, and Butch and his friends were "gettin' all fucked up." He took a swig from his tallboy and continued his story.

"We were standing at the bar talking about the Oakland Raiders or some shit, and I notice these fuckin' fat chicks gigglin' and talkin' about us." Butch's story took a short break as Butch burst into an evil laugh—he frequently sidetracked himself with a drawn out laugh. "So, they keep looking at us, and I tell my buddies, 'These fatties are checkin' us out.' My buds like look over all obvious and shit." Laugh. "Then, like the leader of the fat chicks walks up to us, tryin' to be all sexy like." Laugh. "She's like, 'Do you guys wanna come over and sit with us.' And my friend turns to her and says, 'You fuckin' fat bitch!'" Laugh. "The fat chick gets all upset and tells us to fuck ourselves. We just start crackin' up. So, we stay there for a while, but when we're leavin' the fat chicks are waiting outside the bar for us. It's like a fuckin' herd of fatties. They're like standin' there all pissed, and they wanna fight us. And we're like, 'Fuck off.' But then one of the bitches takes a swing at my bud. He ducks, and the bar has like these stairs that lead up to the bar, he lifts this bitch up and tosses the fat fuck over the ledge." Laughs. My eyes popped wide open in disbelief. He continued after a long laugh. "Then, it turns out into an all out war and fists start gittin' thrown. We just start beatin' the shit outta these fat fuckin' chicks. This one chick comes after me, and I just pull back and smash her right in the face, and her nose like explodes." He laughs as he makes the motions of a nose exploding. "She falls to the ground, and she starts to get up, and I just pull back and Whabaaam! I kick her in the gut. Then one of my friends—I don't know if he ran to the car when we left the bar or what—he comes screechin' up in the car and calls for us, 'Guys, c'mon!' We all jump in and speed off, leaving the fatties just layin' out in front of the bar." Laughs.

Along with his humorous stories, Butch gave information about the treacheries of life. On this particular night, Butch told me about the evils of people. He told me of how people fucked him on several occasions. "People talk behind your back all the time. They fuckin' back stab ya." He said. "There's several people at work who talk about you. They already have talked about you." He motioned at me, and I was taken aback and almost offended. He mentioned someone in particular, and I felt disappointed at the person, and some of the leftover disgust from earlier in the night returned to my veins. Then Butch got real serious and said, "Trust no one, Hakos. I'm serious." I looked at him nodding with a serious glare. "I'm serious." He repeated, feeling as though I was not listening.

"Okay. I know," I assured him.

He later told me of a book some guy wrote that explained the inside workings of fucking with people. He told me to read it because it included things that I could never imagine. It sounded like a good idea. I remember telling my father about it later, and he said, "Do you have to take it to such extremes?" I wondered about that and decided not to read the book. Instead, I decided to leave it to myself to determine people's motives and actions. But I kept Butch's skepticism in the back of my mind.

Butch was a very dynamic character. He flaunted his Italian-American heritage. He also had a military background. He possessed a great confidence, and, most noticeable, Butch had a flailing temper. On certain occasions, he smashed brooms across doors because his employees refused to listen. Other times he screamed at coworkers whom he felt had backstabbed him. During one episode, an employee refused to give Butch a bat that he had ripped away from Butch. Butch chased down the kid and grabbed him by the shirt, pulling him down to the ground. Butch tore the bat away from the defeated kid. The temper never got Butch into any trouble, but it didn't really help his relationship with the employees.

The Guitars employees were mostly adolescent African Americans from the poorer areas of Southtown. They were just kids, working while school was not in session. Like most teenagers, all they wanted was a simple job to get some extra cash. They didn't work especially hard or act especially responsible. But who could blame them? The job stunk. It worked kids too hard. The job expected a lot of commitment and energy—what teenager wants to exert those values during the summer? This makes sense to me today. But back then, it made no sense to me, Butch, or anyone else in the front office. To us, these were punk-ass kids who were lazy. But, again, they were just kids. What did they care about balancing out a register? What did they care if the health inspector docked us because they weren't wearing a hat? They didn't care. Hell, at their age I wasn't even working. What right did I have to judge them? But we did judge them. And we didn't like them, and they didn't like us because we didn't like them.

The whole environment resembled the class structure of pre-Revolutionary France. Al was the King. Below him lived the nobles or clergy—this class consisted of two or three individuals in the front office. Below that was my class—the skilled laborers. These people didn't gain power until the Industrial Revolution. Lastly, there were the lowly peasants. This uneducated mass of people lived a spat-on life. This is the class of our game-day employees. We only used these people for their labor. We exploited them and paid them little.

But in reality, my class and the peasant class had a lot in common. Both of us received little pay and gained little recognition. All of our work was used to fill the coffers of Al. My class never realized how much better things would have been if we would have catered better to the needs of our employees. If only we would have worked together better and made an effort to understand each other, the team would have run much more smoothly. In fact, all the full-time workers, such as myself, needed to do was to evaluate our own situation—when taking our low pay and hours into consideration, we calculated that we earned about $2 an hour, considerably less than our game-day counterparts.

10 CONTINUING HOME STANDS, CONTINUING PROBLEMS MINUS RADIO 40

The next day, I continued my search for radio 40, but it remained a mystery. During my initial search, I arrived at the stadium before most, allowing me time to secretly search while Butch cooked us up some leftovers for breakfast. I always enjoyed a leftover steak from the kitchen and eggs from the Rodriguez brothers. Soon after breakfast, we were back in the stands, cleaning and stocking. In the meantime, locals tried out for the National Anthem, which was always sung by some lucky southerner who wanted to show off their singing abilities. Usually, we mocked the singers. Many stunk, and we were sick of listening to them. Most found it difficult to sing in a stadium environment—the acoustics are rather strange.

 The same day, what was left of the grounds crew failed to show up to work. With such poor oversight of the field, patches of tan death dotted the infield. Who knew how to sod but Butch? Of course; Butch and I had a new job. There we labored in the hot Southtown sun, laying squares of grass in the dried and withered infield. I had never laid sod before. I didn't even know what sod was. Patches of grass in squares? Why? What's the point, I thought. But, I became quite skilled in stapling the blocks of greenery into the ground. After completing the project, I was never quite sure if the sod made the field look any better. Instead of patches of tan death sporadically placed all through the field, there now shined patches of vibrant green, in an otherwise dullish, green field.

As we sodded, the last person trying out to sing the National Anthem was finishing, slowly. She sang the anthem in slow motion, dragging the end of each note off into the distance, where even the Hubble Telescope could see. At least she hit her notes though—some people bounced around the notes of the song without ever really hitting them directly. These were usually cute kids whose parents strongly encouraged them to pursue a singing career. The sloth singer ended, and the stadium sound system, which played the same songs over and over again as if it were a déjà vu machine, resumed play. While I mechanically stapled green grass to dry dirt, my mind wandered to the thought of the coming weekend. With the pounding of annoying classic rock broadcasting from the sound system, I smiled in comfort at the thought of sleeping in on Saturday. It would be the first time in three weeks; somehow, game days kept landing on the weekends. It might have been this glimmer of hope that kept most of this exhausted staff from becoming disgruntled. As long as there was that singular hope of relaxation, I thought little of my abuse.

The schedule left us an entire week without a home game, most of which was spent working the field back to health. The weekend came and went and I spent it lazily, watching television and movies. A weekend is a quick thing, and when most of it is spent sleeping and relaxing, it's even quicker. Sure, some of us would get together for some drinks during our time of freedom, but in reality we all lived quite separately from each other, and most merrymaking took place at the stadium, secretly drinking ourselves away in a concession stand or skybox. Most drinking took place during home stands. No homestand, no fun. A sinister dichotomy.

Monday was the first day of the new home stand—a ruthless thirteen game home stand of cooking and cleaning. As noon approached, I made my way down to the grill to prepare the area and the food. I opened the door to the room that contained the freezer and a wash of the most hideous stench I ever smelled swept past my face. Like the heat of the grill, the scent hurled my body backward, and forced me to double over in disgust. I had never smelled such an odor. I could think that only the smell of a rotting corpse could be anywhere close to this obscenity. I gathered my composure and peeked in the room while holding my mouth with a rag. The sight sickened me almost as much as the smell. For whatever reason, the freezer door hung open, and loads of chicken pieces, drenched in their own blood, lie scattered beneath the opened door. Thousands of maggots undulated in the red pool, causing grotesque, thick ripples to form in the blood. Again, the stench attacked. I stumbled back a couple feet onto the grease-laced floor around the grill. I thought about how the freezer door could have opened up immediately following the last game, leaving the chicken to lie on the floor for eight days, while the Southtown heat baked the room to temperatures well above 140 degrees.

I immediately called Butch, and he rushed down. He ran into the room, but the force of the smell sent his body hurling backwards. He fell to his knees, puking recently eaten nachos.

"What the fuck is that?" he asked with tears in his eyes.

"The freezer door is open. All the chicken's been lying out for days." I thought about how the grounds-keeping work kept us from doing our concessions job during the off week.

"Damn! We gotta open these windows."

Like people walking against the wind in a sandstorm, we ventured into the room and opened the windows. The next job was to wait until the scent died down; however, we couldn't wait too long because of Al. If Al found out about this, we were fucked. We went about, mopping the floor with pure ammonia. The ammonia burnt our nostrils, shredding our smelling sensors. We threw the limp, maggot-ridden pieces of chicken into a trash bag. Butch continued to clean, while I got the pick-up truck and drove the bag off to the trash compactor. When I reached the trash-site, the bag of chicken had over flowed with maggots. Maggots squirmed helplessly around the bed of the truck—the same bed used when receiving cases of food from delivery trucks. I lifted the bag, and reared it back so I could toss it into the dumpster. Upon throwing, the bag ripped open, sending wriggling maggots and rotten chicken all over the trash-site. The smell of death returned, and I bent over with severe nausea. I quickly cleaned up the mess—I am not exactly sure how—I seem to have lost this repulsive memory. I do remember hauling buckets of water back and forth with the hopes of washing away the tragic mess.

As I neared the grill area, I caught the scent of Pine-sol.

"Smells pretty good," I remarked.

"Fuck it. This stuff's awesome. I think we should clean all the concession stands with this shit," Butch answered. Later in the year, when Al was razzing us because of the condition of the concession stands, we took several bottles of Pine-sol and dumped some on the ground. Al came back to inspect, and he said that we did a great job. We never scrubbed a thing.

With the chicken dilemma over on this opening day, I changed gears and began the lighting of the grill. There puffed a constant breeze, which fanned the inside of the grill. The shape and position of the grill created a sort of wind tunnel for any moving air. This made lighting the pilot light difficult. The first pilot light lit easily. The second gave me more of a problem. At first, I thought I had them both lit. But after glancing at the thermometer, I noticed that the heat read only 200 degrees. Confused, I looked inside and saw that the back burners were all out, meaning that the back pilot light was not lit. I ran into the room next door to grab one of our lighters. As I quickly grabbed the lighter, I accidentally flung it across the room, where it landed behind the enormous pizza oven. I fell to the floor and saw the lighter far behind the pizza oven. Rather than struggle for the lighter, I grabbed some matches. I raced back to the grill's ass once more, and I began a long struggle to light the back burners. A breeze persistently blew out my matches. I lit several matches together close to my body in order to get a strong flame. To keep the wind from blowing out the pilot light, I lined the back of the grill with pieces of whatever I could find around the grill. This innovation of a barrier allowed the grill to heat up enough for me to cook. The wind ultimately found gaps in my structure, but I tricked the wind by frequently moving the pieces around—this proved difficult for the wind to figure out, and until the wind realized that it had to completely change its directional current, the man-made blockage provided the burners enough time to cook the dogs and hamburgers with only a slight variation, meaning that the burners were cooking inconstantly because of the force of the wind. This made some burgers in a rack cook while others did not, increasing the problems at the grill—no more set cooking times.

    The lighting problem became one I could deal with as my expertise increased. All attempts to call specialists out to fix the grill fell to utter failure. I always seemed to know more than they did. However, ruined meat products continued to be a problem. I could fix a grill, but I could not fix a rotted piece of chicken. Yes, again with the chicken. We cooked chicken wings that we sent up to the restaurant, which sat atop the stands behind home plate. The chicken had been sitting in the cooler for days, and upon opening the case of 60 wings, I questioned the little buggers' freshness. Again, I called Butch, and he came down to inspect the chicken. He grimaced and thought. I turned my ear closer to him, waiting for a response. "Throw it out?" I asked.

"How many more cases do we have left in the freezer?" he asked.

"None."

Butch thought some more and then uttered, "Cook it." I know it sounds immoral and disgusting that anyone would cook questionable chicken and serve it, but there is another much more important fact: Without every wing, we would not have enough to serve through the night. Without enough to serve, we (Butch mainly) would be strung up by our balls at the top of the stadium entranceway. Al would not have accepted the fact that we allowed cases of chicken to rot away, and, for whatever reason, we actually believed that hiding our failures from Al was more important than serving a mass of bad chicken. It is hard to explain our rationale. Today, I don't understand it, but back then it made sense. So, with the same thought process of somebody living within a totalitarian government where they follow the rules in fear, I looked at Butch, raised an eyebrow, and dumped the sloshy-mix of smelly chicken into the grill. I made sure to cook it a little too long in hopes of killing whatever deathly creature may have been festering within the chicken, and Butch came down to taste test the crap. He took a bite and uttered, "Fuckin' good. Serve it up." We chucked the once-funky chicken into the coolers and sent it up to the concession stands.

Then, I got a call from Mel, "Hakos." I glanced behind me to see Mel fishing around the gutter-like system that wrapped around the grill, draining the excess grease into a grease pit. I walked over to Mel and saw the gutter filled with grease—imagine the gutters on your house completely filled with grease and getting fuller. Before I made any comment, I let out a sigh and rubbed my forehead free of gunk with the back of my hand.

"Why?" I asked.

"It's all backed up," replied Mel.

"Butch," I directed Butch to the problem and asked, "whaddaya think?"

"Fix it," he ran up stairs to tend to other problems.

I turned back to the grill and stared. Just as my brain searched for an antidote, there was a "clunk!" and the rollers inside the grill that moved the racks in circles stopped.

"What?" I asked in utter desperation.

"Id broke, Hakos. Broke," Mel puckered.

I left the grease to overflow onto the cement, while I assessed the broken rollers. The rollers were the bigger problem. The hotdogs could still cook with overflowing grease, but hotdogs could not cook properly when the rotation system broken—that would be a lot of burnt dogs. I flung open the lid, allowing an awful spit of flames to escape, and I checked inside.

"Fuckin' looks fine in there. What the fuck's wrong?" I shouted.

"Hakos." I looked up and saw Mel pointing at the gutter system. The grease had started fire, and it was heading my way like the fuse of a bomb. I leapt backward as the fire skirted by, and I grabbed the hose and shot it at the grill, sending grease and steam everywhere. Some grease sprayed all over the food that sat out on the tables ready to be cooked. However, I had temporarily killed the fire. I stooped around into the freezer room and grabbed a plunger.

"Mel, plunge that grease drain!" I tossed him the plunger, and ran to check on the racks, leaving no one to tend to the cooking.

I examined the grill further and found that a pin that helped rotate the racks had broken away. I thought quickly, and grabbed a nail from inside. I stuck the nail in where the pin had been, burning myself only moderately. This allowed the gears to catch, and the grill started back up. I moved to the back to help Mel with the grease. Then I heard a "clank!" The nail I used snapped. I ran back inside and grabbed a larger nail and shoved it in place of the previous nail. Again, the grill began to roll. I opened the lid and noticed that most of the food was burnt to a crisp. I unloaded several racks and replaced them with uncooked, grease-stained food that was partially brown after sitting in the sun for so long. Then I ran back to help Mel. My face scowled upon seeing this rotund black man caked in grease.

"It ain't workin' Hakos." Again, I turned on my brain, and searched for a solution. A spark flew out from the side of the grill.

"Mel, go watch that food." Mel ran around the grill.

"Hakos, there's a big grease fire!" I ran back to the front and looked inside the grill to see an enormity of a fire. The thermometer read 800 degrees.

"Hose it down," I said to Mel.

He half-laughed, "You know that bad, Hakos."

"It works." I ran back to the clogged drain, and Mel continued to talk through a laugh.

"Oh, Hakos, you crazy. You a crazy man. You tryin' to kill me. That's it. You tryin' to kill me cuz I'm black. You're deescriminatory. Ha! Ha! Deescriminatory!" Mel began laughing while he continued with his claims.

During Mel's raving, I had turned my attention to the grease pit—a container in the ground that supposedly collected all the grease. I had never opened it before, but I figured that it was causing my over flow. Just then, I got drilled by the hose water.

"Ha! Sorry, Hakos."

"No problem. Just get rid of that fire and start cookin'." I could have called for someone over the radio to help me cook the food, but that would have shown that I was having problems, and that would have brought Al down immediately. If he saw this mess, he would have taken that hose and shot it up my ass.

I struggled with the opening of the grease pit, which resembled a sewer lid on the street. I found a broom and tried to lodge the lid free, but the broom snapped in half. Then, I found some miscellaneous metal rod. With great

Sweaty Mascots start Grease Fires

effort and strength, I managed to lift the lid. Grease oozed from the seams, spreading all across the floor around the grill. As I lifted the lid completely, I came face to face with a vat of sludge-like grease—grease so thick that bubbles from below struggled to free themselves at the top.

"Here's the problem, Mel." I turned and noticed that Mel was gone. "Mel." The Guitars had hit a grand slam, and Mel had gone off toward the fence to see the celebration. I ran over to Mel and told him to finish cooking.

"All the food is on," he said.

"Has any come off?"

"No."

"Well, it's probably cooked don't you think?"

He puckered up and agreed, "Probly so, Probly so."

Mel continued to pull off cooked food, while replacing the spaces on the grill with uncooked food. Most of the food coming off was cooked unevenly, but that was not an issue at this particular moment. Instead, I turned back to the grease. I came up with a plan to shovel the grease-sludge into a trashcan. I shoveled and shoveled, wanting desperately to ask one of my runners to help, but they were only 16 years old, and I didn't want them to get injured. Finally, I broke. "Mel! Come shovel this." He gave me an adolescent look of disappointment and apathy. I repeated with a roar, "Mel, shovel this now!" He sulked over and started shoveling the crap into the trashcan.

I ran over to help Mel and attempted to organize everything back to normal.

Just then, Woofman appeared.

"Hey, ahh, this place looks like shit. Throw me one of them sausages." Woofman bit off more than half of the sausage. "You know if Al saw this, he'd have your ass. Damn it's hot out here." Woofman made an art out of changing conversational directions to the point of absolute nonsense. "You guys got any of those pops down here?"

"Yeah, in there." I blurted while still attempting to organize the cooking situation.

Woofman made one last disgusted glance at the area, and he walked into the freezer room to grab a soda.

"Hey, Hakos!" Woofman shouted. I ran into the room. "This is what ya aughtta do." He cracked open a pop and walked into the cooler (the cooler was quite large). "C'mon." Confused, I followed, and Woofman sat his sweaty ass on some cases of hotdogs and enjoyed the cool air. He was a large man, and the heat, plus walking, was apparently getting to him. His face was beet red. He sighed and looked into space. I stood in the cooler waiting for some enlightening comment from the mouthy giant who dragged me into the cooler. After a few moments of watching him stare off into Blissville, I shrugged with frustration, and left him in the cooler. Strange fucker, I thought to myself.

Butch visited the grill to see how things were going. I asked him how the chicken wings were, and he said people were eating them up like crazy. Just then, a voice on the radio called for me, wondering why the dogs in stand two were all crusty and burnt. This contrasted immensely with the radio call from stand three that said that their dogs were raw. Butch's face contorted, and he damned the stand's pleas.

"Why the fuck do they call that shit over the radio? I was just up there," Butch bitched.

"Fuck." This was the only reply I could think of.

"Hakos, what's going on down there?" Al shouted on the radio.

"Shit," Butch and I said this jointly on cue as if practiced.

"We're checkin' on it," Butch replied.

"Well, fix it!" Al shouted back. "Is everything alright?"

"I'm checkin'," I answered.

"It either is or it isn't!" Al barked.

"Yeah, it's fine," Butch insisted. Butch turned to me and told me that he was going to go up to the stands and fix the problems from there. I was to fix the problems at the grill.

"Al's on a run today," Mel interjected. I merely raised my eyebrows. My brain was too scattered to send a message to my mouth to verbally acknowledge Mel's comment. "Dat ain't good, Hakos. You know?" Mel continued. I nodded. He went on, "You can't do that to your workers. It ain't right. It ain't right."

"He's the boss, I guess." This was my only response as I my mind focused on the grill.

"You know what I am, huh? Hakos? You know what I am? Al's nigga." Mel began to laugh hysterically. "Al's nigga." Mel's antics caused me to forget about the current situation. I busted out laughing as well. Mel continued on, "Al's nigga," he said this several more times. "Just call me blacky, Hakos. Nothin' I can do about it." He started scrubbing his arm, "It don't come off. I'm a black man the rest of my life! I can't wash it off."

"And you can call me Whitey."

Mel exploded into a jittery dance of hilarity. "Whitey!" For the moment, we had forgotten about the battlefield of grease around us. It was just a couple of guys enjoying each other's company.

"You gotta laugh about it, Hakos. That's the only way to talk about it. You white and I'm black."

"You're right, Mel."

"It ain't good to hold it inside. That ain't what the good Lord wants you to do. We are here to be joyful and laugh. You know...Jesus was a black man."

I laughed more. "That's bull. He was a whitey."

"Oh boy, Hakos. Praise the Lord. Praise the Lord. Don't listen to him Jesus. We knows you a black man."

The joking went on for a while. I had never actually joked with a black man about race, especially religious race. I realized Mel could be right—race had to be made into an open joke. It seemed the only way to turn such a tabooed subject into an accepted everyday topic. Only by laughing about it could any two people get on the same side about the subject. Here were two underpaid grill boys discussing race with ease. Mel had opened up to me, and I accepted his humor and opened up to him. Though I still didn't trust Mel alone at the grill, I trusted him as a human. He was a poor black man, who worked several jobs, but he loved life, and he knew the meaning of it. I had graduated from college and had come from a well-off family. Mel had no real formal education, and he came from the poorer side of Southtown; however, Mel had accepted life as it was, and I was struggling with it. All the problems such as undercooked hotdogs and a broken grill sickened me. My body tensed up with fear. On the other hand, Mel took each dilemma in stride, and he seemed unfazed by events that I took as catastrophes. He enjoyed each moment, and he emitted a glow of joy. As I stood there laughing, assessing the two of us, I could not help thinking of death. Which of us will be happier when we die? I thought of myself lying there thinking back to all the times when I grew tense with fear. Will I be mad at myself in the end for always tensing up when in a crunch? Would I think I wasted my time dwelling on fright and terror, when at the same time I could have been laughing with delight? Sure I could dread each moment, but I could also enjoy each moment. What's the point of dread? Mel seemed to be immune to dread. When he dies, he will think back on years of smiling and laughing, even when the going was tough. I saw myself disappointed on my deathbed because of wasted time with thoughts of fear, and I saw Mel smiling on his deathbed, knowing that he lived each moment with a smile. Whatever the philosophy, at this moment, we were two men enjoying a good laugh. Sure, the grill was still breaking, and the fire was still raging inside the grill, but we breezed through the rest of the night with a sense of lightheartedness.

Butch ventured up into the concession stands to get a handle on things. He yelled at the stand managers for calling us out over the radio. He told them to relay their grievances to him, and he would fix the problem. The dogs in stand three were cold—we had run out of thawed dogs and we were trying to cook frozen dogs, which had to be pried apart due to the ice that had formed around them. This made an interesting combination of having frozen hands and burnt hands all in the same minute. Butch found that stand two had set their warmers on too high, which meant that the dogs inside were drying out and burning; not to mention the plastic wrap around the hotdog was melting onto the bun.

Before closing down the grill, I thought about Woofman. I wondered if he left the cooler without me knowing. I walked into the freezer room and opened the cooler slowly. There he sat still drinking a soda, only now he munched on a raw hotdog. I don't think he noticed me, so I closed the door and snuck away.

The next night was more of the same. The pilot light went out several times, while a runner shoveled grease into the trashcan. Frozen food came out cold in the middle. Racks fell on the greasy ground along with hotdogs, hamburgers, and chicken breasts, all of which were cooked and served. Woofman visited us and made stupid-ass comments. Stand managers called us out again and again, and Al swore over the radio, making it uncomfortable for those with radios to stand next to patrons. Meanwhile, Mel comforted me with his carefree style. At one point, I noticed the thermometer on the grill reading 200 degrees. The pilot light had gone out.

"Shit!" I cried.

"That grill ain't hot, Hakos," Mel told me. Mel often informed me of happenings after the fact.

"I know. The pilot light is out again." I squatted down on the greasy floor, crumpling my body in such a way so as to fit my hands into the beast. I relit the pilot light, and Mel and I continued racking the food.

"You know what we gotta call this grill, Hakos, don't ya?"

"What?"

"Hitler." I smiled, somewhat surprised and confused. But then I figured that he was referring to the fact that the grill was this enormous Auschwitz-like fire chamber. I thought the name crude, but I understood the meaning. But Mel continued, "You know why we call it Hitler, don't ya?"

"Why?" I asked, expecting the Auschwitz answer.

"Because you know what Hitler was don't ya?"

"What?"

"A dictator! And that's what this grill does. It dictates whether or not it's gonna work every night." Mel ruptured into a frenzied laugh. I grinned. Mel's rationale caught me off guard. I thought Mel was going to talk about gas chambers and fiery ovens, but instead, he devised this rather clever explanation. Mel continued to laugh, calling the grill a dictator. And I agreed to call the grill Hitler.

As Mel and I laughed about Hitler, a strangely formed black man entered the grill area. He stood taller than Mel and wore glasses with lenses so think they resembled magnifying glasses. The glasses were layered with smeared muck. His pinstriped shorts were jacked up past his oversized belly, and his socks did the same over his calves. He wore a Guitars ball cap, and greeted me with, "Hey, friend."

"Hello." I was a bit confused. I didn't know this character or why he was at the grill.

"Hey, Mel."

"Hello." Mel turned to me, "Hakos, this is my brother." Mel turned back to his brother, "What are you doing here?"

"I...I...I," apparently, Mel's brother suffered from a severe stuttering problem. In attempting to articulate his words, Mel's brother contorted his face and motioned his hands as if trying to pull the words from his mouth, "I...burgers, man. Burgers."

"Why you need burgers?" Mel asked.

"Team, man, the...the...team, needs 'um man."

Usually, we cooked food for the team if they had not ordered something else to eat—this was their dinner.

"How many burgers?" Mel asked.

Mel's brother almost growled out, "Don't know, man. Don't know."

"Does he take food to the club house?" I asked Mel.

"Yeah, he's the clubby."

"Clubby, man. I... I...I...I, the clubby, man," Mel's brother stuttered.

A voice shouted over the radio, "Hakos, I just sent Partner over to the grill to pick up a bout fifty hamburgers. Just put them in a pan and send 'um back with Partner."

I looked up at Mel's brother, "Your name is Partner?"

He grinned, showing his few teeth, and growled, "Yeah." He laughed a little.

I turned to Mel, "Why is his name Partner?"

"He used to just call people Partner. Now everyone else calls him Partner."

"Alright. Alll...right, friend," Partner blurted. He smiled and put his hand on my shoulder, saying, "You a trip, man. You a trip."

I wasn't sure why I was a trip, but I smiled and loaded a pan with hamburgers. Partner waddled away in his pinstripe shorts.

Again, many hotdogs strategically maneuvered their way through our rushed hands and onto the greasy concrete. On many occasions, in response to the dropped hotdogs, I said, "What you don't know won't hurt you." I simply picked the dog up from the filthy ground, twirled it in my hand like a shiny six-shooter—a trick learned from handling billions of hotdogs—and tossed the wiggly wiener into the rack for cooking. This night saw a lot of dropped hotdogs for whatever reason. Both Mel and I had butterfingers. On one occasion, Mel ripped open a case of hotdogs, causing some dogs to explode out of the box. We scrambled to grab the damn things, but several of them used their nimble squirming to escape our slick gloved hands. The dogs dropped to the greasy ground and bounced madly upon impact. They rolled and skipped about the ground as if they were trying desperately to escape the treachery of Hitler. We caught most of them, and we placed them into the racks.

Mel looked up at me with an enlightened air and said, "Whatcha don't know, ya don't know."

I knew what he meant, and I didn't want to laugh at him so I stifled my laugh and agreed, "That's right. Whatcha don't know, ya don't know." This became the philosophy of the grill.

Most of what occurred at the grill took place in secrecy. For instance, the Southtown area was swarming with a cicada population of Biblical proportions. These seemingly untrained flying creatures fluttered everywhere. By their numbers, it was as though they competed against oxygen for airspace percentage. Cicadas surpassed peanut shells as the most populated piece of trash, and sweeping hundreds of cicada carcasses was a stomach churning experience. I don't know if God was trying to speak to us—Mel thought so—but I do know that these prehistoric insects were everywhere. The most stunning aspect of a cicada is that they have wings but they really cannot fly. They kind of fart around the air, bumping into everything. They are like a carbon-based knuckle ball. My biggest fear was that they made sanitation a difficult process. These things got caught in the cooking racks, and they got cooked up with the rest of the food. It was impossible to avoid. Many committed suicide by flying straight into Hitler while he was opened. Some ended their lives by splashing into the boiling juice that the hotdogs dipped into while in Hitler. Needless to say, during the summer of 1997, people in Southtown ate hotdogs basted in cicada juices.

The racks themselves also presented a case of barf-causing foulness. These metal cages collected a great deal of meat particles throughout the night. Therefore, we painstakingly scrubbed them down in a washbasin behind the grill. Sometimes we let them soak in the soap because the grime was so intense. We got those damn racks spotless. Unfortunately, between home stands, something happened with the racks. Perhaps it was some super hero-like metamorphosis. I'm not sure. What I am sure about is the fact that when we opened the bins that contained the racks after a home stand, we noticed something quite peculiar. Some sort of fuzzy fungus appeared on parts of the racks. I still don't know what this stuff was, but it was disgusting. No worries though, usually we didn't use the racks that grew mold.

There were many other catastrophes outside the concession life. Woofman, who struggled with a bit of egoism, believed that, even though he was a dog trainer, he also possessed a superior knowledge of maintenance and tooling. His arrogant demeanor transcended all areas of life. Such a mindset created problems and arguments between Woofman and everybody else. The most apparent of these problems included the man hired to do the maintenance work, Hamm.

Al hired Hamm to do all the daily repairs of the stadium, a full-time job, to say the least. However, the fact that Al, an eccentric perfectionist from the North, hired a slow-paced, Gomer-like Southerner baffled me. The two never saw eye-to-eye, and Hamm caused more problems than he was worth. Hamm was an AWOL goofball whose experience in maintenance work was rather limited—he had a tool belt and some drills, but he really lacked any sense that could be used to determine what to fix and what to leave alone. It was this rather expert stupidity that brought Hamm into conflict with Woofman on a daily basis. If Hamm was called to a job over the radio, Woofman showed up to the job as well.

"That stupid fuck ass. He was fixing a fuckin' light fixture in one of the concession stands and dropped the fuckin' thing on the floor. Glass fuckin' flew everywhere," Woofman informed me. He enjoyed calling Hamm out on his failures. Hamm's constant butterfingers didn't help his quest to gain respect. Actually, he was completely oblivious to the lack of respect he received from the staff—the man failed to realize the thoughts and comments of others around him. He failed to realize much of anything.

Al fired Hamm three separate times because of Hamm's addiction to folly. The first time came during one of our biggest games of the season. It was a full-house Saturday afternoon game. The staff needed to be at the stadium by seven o'clock in order to get the stadium beautified and readied for the game. As eight o'clock rolled around, we had all built up a supreme sweat from working at the stadium. I entered the main office to order some additional cases of beer and witnessed an all out motherfucking by Al.

"Where the fuck is that guy?" Al screamed, referring to Hamm.

Woofman egged Al on saying, "He was supposed to fix the lights on the scoreboard."

All of a sudden, Hamm appeared, chewing on a jelly donut. He really was enjoying his donut, and he smiled with delight as he said, "Hey guys, wassup?"

Al's eyes turned as red as the fires building inside of him, "Where the fuck have you been? You were supposed to be here at seven!" The office stood still as Al motherfucked Hamm. That was the first time Hamm was fired.

Later, Hamm reappeared. I am not sure why, but I believe it was because Woofman couldn't do all the maintenance work because of his traveling dog show. Soon after his restoration, we heard a large crash in the parking lot. Hamm stumbled into the office with his face covered in blood. When asked what had happened, Hamm couldn't recount anything—he stood dazed beyond reality. Apparently, Hamm, again late for work, came screaming through the parking lot in his car, swerving through the parked cars. Unfortunately, the starting pitcher for that night and his family were also traveling through the parking lot. Hamm smashed his little red car into the family's van. Though all were shaken up a little, Hamm was the only one injured. And fired.

Nevertheless, Al rehired the mindless Hamm one last time. When called to fix some plumbing, Hamm met Woofman who was already working on the plumbing problem. The two got into an argument, initiated by Woofman's instigating tendencies. The argument developed into a full-fledged fight, culminating with Woofman lifting Hamm up into the air by the neck—that was the final end of feeble Hamm, and the first time I had ever seen a man lift another man by the neck.

BIT 11: CHICAGO AND THE MEANING OF LIFE

One time, I told Al about the problems down at the grill. I told him how things did not always work.

"Well, we can't have that, huh," Al said.

"I've been able to handle it so far," I answered.

"Well, yeah, but we can't have that blow up in our face some night," he replied with crooked eyebrows.

Al instructed me to call someone out who might be able to fix the grill. I walked back to my air-conditioned concessions office and slammed the phone book onto my desk. As I scanned the various people who worked maintenance on grills and similar items, I wondered if they would be able to do the job. I imagined Hitler scaring the man away with an intimidating roar. It's not as though Hitler was your usual backyarder. Finally, I got a hold of some guy named Topopolis who worked on grills. I waited for him in the office, and when he and his accomplice arrived, I led him down to Hitler. As soon as they entered, I could not keep my eyes off the accomplice, a Greek guy with an enormous mustache. He clumsily looked around as he stepped about with his clunky shoes. When we reached Hitler, the boss took a phone call. That left me with the mustachioed man who spoke no English. I stood and watched as Mustache Man set down the case he had been carrying. He unlatched the locks and opened the case to reveal a whole lot of stuff that looked like a little kid's scientist set. The man took out what looked like something that measures rainfall. He partially filled it with water and examined it closely. He held it right to his nose. I looked at him in wonder. He breathed a heavy breath as he concentrated on his water. He then set his water gauge down and scrambled through his mess of tools, breathing ever heavier. He searched for some time until he found some slender piece of metal. He picked back up his rain gauge and held it close to his face again. Now, he tapped it with his metal strip. What is he doing?, I thought. Just then, the boss came around the counter and began ordering him in a loud abrasive Greek tone. The boss ordered Mustache Man to put his water gauge away and focus on the grill, at least that is what I thought he said. In the end, Topopolis and his mustached friend rigged some metal covers around the pilot light so that the wind would not blow out the flame. This worked minimally.

I told Al of the Greeks, and he replied with, "The fuck." I could tell he was skeptical of the new "wind blockers." I assured him that they would help. However, Al insisted on perfection. In one case, one of the representatives of the maker of Hitler flew down to see how the dictator was handling himself. I told the representative about some of the problems, but he seemed more worried about our technique than anything else. When told of the pilot lights, he said, "Yeah, that happens to us also when we're cooking, but you just light it back up."

"Well, yeah, I do that, but it might go out again. Isn't there anyway that I could keep it from going out?" I asked.

"Really, you got the grill in the wrong place. You got these prevailing winds streaming in this little gulch here."

Now, Hitler weighed as much as a blue whale; did the guy really think I was going to move it? He quickly changed the topic.

"You guys gotta clean those burners in there better. Are you getting unequal cooking?"

"Yeah."

"That's why. You really gotta scrub those."

"Well, if the burners go out, then the whole thing cooks unevenly."

"They're going out cuz they're clogged from the excess grease."

This might have been so, but the burners went out more from the pilot light not working. This bastard just made it seem as though it was my fault Hitler was on the fritz. This is Hitler we're talking about!

The answers and help I got from the outside proved to me that only I knew Hitler. Only I knew the special way to rig the pilot light. Only I knew how to rig it so that it might cook evenly. Only I knew everything about this grill. I forgot calling for any more help. I decided to do it myself from then on.

Still, that didn't prevent Al from wanting perfection. Al wanted Butch and me to be a successful concessions crew. I would have to say we were doing quite well, considering neither one of us had any experience. However, Al wanted expert concession people. Therefore, he sent Butch and me to our sister team up in the north (we had the same owners) for the weekend to learn from their concessions crew. Al was general manager with this team before he made the trip down to Southtown. Basically, everyone who worked for our northern counterpart worked for Al previously.

It was a 6:30 a.m. flight. I picked Butch up at 5:15 a.m., and we ate a quick breakfast. We traveled to the airport and boarded our plane. Butch chose the back of the plane.

"You know why you pick the back of the plane?" He asked me.

"Why?"

"So when the plane crashes, you're the last to go." He said this while using his hands to illustrate the crash.

I never was really high on flying, and Butch's comment persuaded me to study the safety instructions manual. While looking through the cartooned instructions, Butch looked over from the back seat and pointed out a particular character on the manual who floated in the water with his seat cushion.

"He's fuckin' stoned," Butch joked. I laughed and looked closer to see that the character's expression did look a little glazed. To this day, I look for all the stoned cartoon characters on the airplane's safety cards—takes up a good five to seven minutes of air time.

We reached our destination and noticed a limo driver holding a card that read "Guitars." We were surprised and gave each other a curious look. We jumped in the back of the limo, and we immediately raised the barrier between the driver and us. We didn't look like the typical limo-riders. We wore baseball caps, tennis shoes, and t-shirts. The long morning didn't help our appearance either. We took off our shoes and lounged in the back of the limo. We had a 45-minute drive ahead of us. Butch fell asleep, and I stared out the window.

Finally, we reached the stadium. Butch wiped the drool from his mouth and shirt. The driver helped us out of the car, and we stumbled with red eyes and unlaced tennis shoes; our shoes dragged against the ground as we walked. We staggered through the front door and greeted an attractive receptionist. She announced our arrival, and, the rest of the day, we exerted the least amount of effort in our concessions experience. This team owned vehicles devoted especially to the concessions effort. They had a forklift! And there were more than just two concessions employees. We saw how easy the job could be. We made the most of our first day, and the concessions director gave us some beer to take back to our hotel room. We wanted to drink, but we instantly passed out from exhaustion.

We woke the next day and went through the same "easy" routine. I spent most of my time on their outdoor grill, which really was a charcoal burning grill—not like my beastly gas monster back in Southtown.

During our stay, we had become acquainted with a couple of girls who we persuaded to go out with us. They introduced us to some country music/techno bar. While Butch drank and macked on his chick, I wildly danced with my girl. Together we jumped around the entire dance floor, winding in and out of other dancers. We put on great routines and mimicked those dancers who really couldn't dance. We danced for about two hours, and, finally, we laughed our way off the dance floor, joking about our idiocy. As we walked off the dance floor, a tall gentleman accosted us. He wore a strange expression, and I wondered what his intentions were. Then he spoke.

"I just want to thank you guys." This was not what I expected out of his mouth. The smile still stretched across my face from all of our laughing, but the man's sincerity confused me.

"You saved my life," he said with all seriousness.

"Oh, yeah?" I giggled, and I looked at the girl who laughed even harder.

"I had planned to kill myself tonight." We both continued to giggle, though I tried to contain it.

Is he joking?, I thought.

Our laughing did not phase the man's sincere effort; it only encouraged him to talk more. He began to cry, and each word he spoke was accompanied by an attempt to keep tears back. "Tonight, I was going to kill myself." His sincerity finally brought my laughing to an end. I began to feel sorry for the man. The girl continued to laugh, and I periodically looked over at her and smiled. The man continued, "Tonight, I found my wife with another man. She's been cheating on me. And it just tore my heart out. I felt a complete loss to go on living."

"Nah, don't think that," I said.

"Yeah, you can go on," the girl said, still attempting to hold back her giggles.

The man continued to talk over our simple efforts of encouragement. "I've lived with my wife for so long. I still love her, you know. I love her. And when I saw her with another man, I just couldn't handle it. I've been sitting over there drinking and just trying to decide what to do. Then, when I saw you two dancing around, having so much fun, I knew there was more to life."

"Yeah, don't kill yourself. It's not worth it." We were not motivational speakers, but we thought we needed to persuade him to live by providing some vocal support.

"I just want to thank you," the man said as we shrugged off the compliments. "You have given me something to live for. I'm not going to kill myself tonight."

"Or any night," I interjected. I thought it was important for him to make a permanent pact not to kill himself.

"No, I won't." He placed his hand on my shoulder. "Thank you." The man walked off into the darkness. We looked at each other and let loose a little giggle, but, in reality, I felt overwhelmed. Wow. Did that really happen? Was it serious? Do we have the power to do what the man said we did? It felt great that we had helped someone find a reason to live. All we were doing was enjoying life, and it was enough of a model to encourage someone to smile through a tragedy.

It was about 3 a.m. We grabbed Butch and his girl, and we drove off for the hotel—our plane left at 6:30 a.m. The girls dropped us off, and as they pulled away, I quickly bent over and gave my girl a kiss.

"I would have been disappointed if I wouldn't have done that," I said awkwardly.

"That's ok," she said with a smile and drove off.

I walked back into the hotel and noticed Butch passed out in the lobby. I decided to sit with him and wait for our cab, which was coming in 45 minutes. We made it to the airport, boarded the plane, and traveled straight to the stadium where we began another day of labor-intensive work, on no sleep.

During our lunch, which we seldom took since we had no time, Butch and I took a pit stop in our office. I slid under my desk into my makeshift bed and took a 20-minute nap, while Butch lit a cigarette and reclined. When I woke, Butch was gone. I was in the concessions office all by myself. After my nap, I felt rejuvenated, and my head was clear. I took time to think of our trip to the North. I smiled at our craziness, and I thought fondly of the man whose life we saved. With a clear head, I thought about a wide array of issues. One issue in particular entered my thoughts—radio 40. Only two other people shared the office with Butch and me; one of these was Woofman. I never trusted the Woof. I snuck over to his desk and examined some of the useless objects that littered his desk. I read the unimportant reminders that he scratched on his desk calendar. Fucking Woof, I thought. At the moment, he was outside with his dog. They were practicing stunts and skits for the game. I thought to myself that he probably took my radio. "Maybe he lost his radio, and he's been using mine all this time." I pulled open some drawers and looked under some soiled fat-man clothes. I opened a drawer that was behind his desk. The Radio! In the desk lay a radio among a litter of scrap paper. I picked up the radio and turned it over to read the number. Shit! Radio 39. It was not radio 40. By this time, I had pretty much given up hope of ever finding my radio, but I kept the search alive. In the heads of everyone else, I was to blame. But I wanted to prove my innocence. I was the Fugitive and the radio my One-Armed Man. Woofman's purity pissed me off. I wanted to get back at him for not being the one who stole my radio. I searched my brain and his desk for an answer. There, glimmering in the light, it showed itself to me. There, alone on this desk, sat a tack. Yes. The tack was on my side. I could tell. Woofman left the tack behind without putting it to any use. I looked at Woofman's pin board and thought that the lonely tack could actually be pinned up without much effort; however, the tack merely sat rolling in circles like tacks do. I knew the tack was on my side, and I sought revenge for the tack and my frustrated self. I picked up the tack and rubbed it with pleasing assurance. I saw the tack agree to my plan. I saluted the tack and carefully placed the martyr on Woofman's seat with the pointy side facing up. Hah. We got this bastard.

I jumped back under my desk just in time. Woofman burst into the room. I tried to peak at him through a crack under my desk.

"Hey, ahh, Hakos. Get out here." The bastard spotted me after a squinted effort.

"Yeah?" I crawled out into the open just as he sat into his chair. Apparently, the tack had no effect—too much ass-blubber, I guessed.

"Ya ever freebase?" asked an over-heated Woof.

"What? Umm, no." I've always found it difficult to answer questions that come from nowhere.

"Well, this heat reminds me of freebasin'."

"Yeah."

"First you get a spoon, and ya put the shit in there, and then you start burnin' the shit with a lighter or some shit. Then you inject that shit hot into your blood. It's crazy shit. Fuck. I'm so fuckin' hot right now, I feel like the burnin' shit. Ya ever try the shit?"

Again, "Nah."

"You should try it, Hakos."

"I don't know. I'll stick to the beer, I guess."

"I could use a cold..." He stopped and a concerned look appeared on his face. His body began to shift. Finally, he raised his ass and felt underneath his rotund butt. He pulled out the tack. "What the fuck. I thought I felt something stabbin' my ass." I couldn't help but laugh. "Hakos, you fuck." He threw the tack at me and laughed along with me. Then, a stern scowl swept over his face. "I'll get you back." He stomped out of the room, leaving me wide-eyed and ill at ease, but still laughing.

Will he get me back? Will he fuck me? I wondered these petty questions, but, at the moment, I laughed in my little desk-bed about my whimsical scheme.

12 CHICAGO SWINGS IN

In Al's constant attempt to build a perfect concessions crew, a couple of the guys from Chicago flew down to give us a hand and show us how we could improve. Ralph, the head of the Chicago concessions crew, led the way in helping us organize our stands and warehouse better. We took inventory thousands of times, and we analyzed all of our purchases. When Al found out that Butch had been ordering a cheaper "all-meat" hotdog, he went up in flames.

"All meat! You know what's in that shit?" Al screamed.

"It's cheaper," Butch insisted.

"Lips and hearts and any shit they fuckin' grind up! That's it! Ralph, get in there and fix this shit up!" Al barked.

We did learn a lot from Ralph. He was a spastic Armenian who never quit moving, but even he found it difficult to make the concessions work. In Chicago, everything was at his disposal, and they had the latest in technology to assist them. With the Guitars, he worked in an archaic system. He stayed for a couple of games and got us organized. He worked relentlessly, but unlike Butch and me, Ralph took hour lunches.

It was suggested that we go to the local booby-joint for lunch. Interestingly enough, the booby-joint served a lovely buffet between the hours of 11 a.m. and 3 p.m. With naked tits shaking in our face and slender legs wrapping around shiny poles, we ate a rather delicious lunch. It was a strange experience, but for whatever reason, it seemed normal. Glasses and silverware clanked just like in any restaurant, but in this joint, women flaunted their boobies. After scarfing down our chocolate pudding cake, Ralph decided he wanted a lap dance. The thought became an obsession with him. He grabbed the attention of one of the girls, and he bargained his way into a two-for-one deal.

"Who wants a lap dance with me?" Ralph shouted.

Everybody looked around, hoping that someone else would speak out. Nobody wanted this going on their record. I started to rationalize; Al wanted me to learn from the best concessions guy. I would only be following Ralph's lead. This would make me a better concessions worker.

"I'll go," I said with a shrug of the shoulders.

"Okay, let's go, Hakos," Ralph said, motioning his hand for me to come. He looked up at the girl again and asked, "Two-for-one, right?" The girl nodded. The others all laughed as the girl escorted Ralph and me to the back.

She sat us down, side by side, on a couch. She spread our legs so that our knees touched.

"This is pretty weird, Hakos. I've never done this with another man before."

"Me neither."

"I hope not."

The girl began sliding her body across ours; first Ralph, then me. She rotated her ass in our crotches and slinked her boobies across our faces. She rubbed her thighs on our cheeks, and dipped her naked crotch to our noses. I looked over at Ralph and saw him shoot his tongue out.

The whole thing ended quickly. Ralph paid the girl, and we walked back. Ralph grabbed me by the neck and said, "Her legs were prickly. She didn't shave. What the fuck's up with that?"

We reached the others and walked outside, a half hour late for work. Ralph began laughing and saying, "I licked her clit! Hakos, did she stuff her cunt in your face?"

"Yeah."

"Did you lick it?"

"No."

"I licked her clit!"

"You're gonna get a disease from that," someone suggested.

"I don't care. Her legs were spiky. We'll probably contract something from her hairy legs!"

BIT 13: RADIO 40 (SOLVED)

The next day, I stood at the grill going through the motions to get everything right (or at least not fuck up too much). Ralph and his crew had already flown back to Chicago. Mel Belle, who was late, hopped down the stairs, praising God. Here, on a day that was too hot with a grill that was too broken, Mel seemed to skip through the daises and believed all was well. He approached the dreaded grill with a smile and screamed loves to the Lord. I simply looked at Mel and smiled before jumping back into the frustrated cooking of dogs and hamburgs. How does he do it? I wondered about his holiness and spirituality. I couldn't figure it out, but I began to believe that Mel's values were purer than mine. He was truly blessed.

More dog droppings and unsanitized surfaces occurred throughout the rest of the summer. My only goal was to create an illusion of concession perfection. I followed Butch's demands, and together we secured a concessions department that demanded respect from every other Guitars employee. Together, Butch and I were known as the hardest workers on Earth.

The last barrier keeping us from a complete state of grace was the health inspector. When I heard that she had finally come to the stadium, my stomach conducted sinister laboratory-like experiments, producing an unmatched amount of diarrhea build-up. Holy shit! Each game day, we wondered if the health inspector might show. The thought crept about in the back of my head every day. Much of what we did was against regulations. When I received the call on the radio, "Hakos, the health inspector is here," I quickly ordered my workers to clean up the area and put gloves on their hands. I told them to get rid of the beverages they were drinking. I hastily took the coolers full of food around an undetectable corner—according to regulations, transporting the food in coolers like ours was not acceptable. We cleaned the area like raging madmen. Unfortunately, our open-air cooking setup broke health code standards—some form of roofing was mandatory (might have helped with the cicadas). Basically, there was nothing we could do to make the area sanitary. In my attempt to make it sanitary, I opened containers of whatever soap I could find. We used so much soap that the whole area looked like a bubble bath. The place may have been damn clean at that point, but hotdogs with soapsuds dripping from them were just as unsanitary as anything I had before. I imagined the agony Butch was going through up in the concession stands as he guided the health inspector around the stadium. I felt a throbbing ticking of a clock in my head as I waited for their arrival. How the hell can we clean this in time? Every time someone walked down the stairs to the grill, I thought it was Butch and the health inspector. But they never came. Luckily, Butch outsmarted the health inspector and never showed our cooking machine. When the health inspector asked to see the commissary, Butch took her to an unused concession stand. She took the bait, and our filthy stadium passed with flying colors. I think Butch even got a date with her.

The day after the last game of the season was like heaven. A huge weight had been lifted off my shoulders. I didn't have to worry about cooking temperatures or lighting Hitler. Our only job now was to clean. Throw me a bottle of Pine-sol!

Strange news came this day though. As I was leaving, a couple of employees were talking at the front desk. I stopped to listen, and they told me that the grounds crew mysteriously disappeared earlier in the season because they were in a car accident and died. I thought about the two kids for a moment and felt awfully sorry for them. However, one of the kid's mothers brought some of the stuff back to the stadium that belonged to the Guitars. One of the items found with the dead bodies was radio 40. Radio 40! I knew it! I knew I had not lost it! I knew someone stole the fucker! I told everyone off, and then I thought about the kids driving down the street, playing with radio 40. This was probably the distraction that took their minds off the road long enough to get into an accident and die. For a second, I thought maybe I caused their death because I had left radio 40 somewhere, and some fucker stole it. But after a few seconds of this thought, I brushed it off as bogus, and I went back to praising the day after the season.

The thought of not having to worrying about cooking dogs excited me. Wow! What freedom! Is this what the realization of freedom and liberty feels like? It's wonderful to feel so liberated. Utterly fantastic. No longer did I have to worry about my strenuous cooking job.

Unfortunately, it was my turn to talk to Al. At the end of the season, Al conducted end of the season reviews on each employee. Al never had anything against me—I was merely a grill boy who did his job. Al knew that I was still a youngster, but I could tell that he could never figure me out. I drove a BMW, but I was able to put up with the hell of Hitler. I could tell this confused Al, who enjoyed working "silver-spooned" kids to the point of quitting. Also, my inability to say anything of any significance really threw him for a loop. On the contrary, he was Al, and there was nothing I could do that would trump his hand. But this was fine, since I had no intention of upstaging Al.

Sweaty Mascots start Grease Fires

I was willing to work any job for the Guitars, and Al needed a go-getter like me.

I sat down across from Al and he said, "So, how's the clean up going?"

"Fine."

"Oh, yeah?"

"Yeah."

"You like working here?"

"Yeah."

"Oh, yeah?"

"Yeah."

"I've been impressed with your work."

"Oh, yeah?" I had adopted the phrase.

"Yeah. When you first came in here, I was like, 'Who is this guy?' What the fuck is that you drive? A Mercedes?" I did not correct him. I think my ability to let people believe wrong facts about me was another trait of mine that threw Al for a loop. "I know you haven't had the most..." he paused, looking for a word.

"Glamorous job?" I interjected.

"Well, no. But you haven't gotten to do a lot of the work you came here for, like group sales. But you've done a good job with what you've been given." I felt good about his comments. It was nice to know that he realized the hard work I had been doing. "Do you wanna to stay here?"

"Yeah. Of course."

"Oh, yeah?"

"Yeah."

"Well, I don't know where I'm going to place you. Maybe the reading program. But we'll talk about that later. Alright, get back to work."

I went back to cleaning the concessions with a cheery attitude. It was nice to be complimented, especially by Al. I knew he thought that I was kind of quirky, but the fact that he made the effort to say something nice was huge—especially coming from Al. So, there I stood, in concession stand two, shooing away the cockroaches. I opened a bottle of Pine-sol and dumped a few dribbles onto the floor.

All the concessions equipment had to be organized by stand and stored. It was a time-consuming process, but it was also stress free. Sure, we had to clean popcorn makers, hotdog warmers, nacho cheese machines, bratwurst rollers, barbeque warmers, pretzel rotators, ice cream mechanisms, beer and keg coolers, steam tables, condiment carts, cold plates, beer hose lines, portable beverage carts, tables and their cloths, chairs, and whatever else was made for the purpose of aiding ingestion, but it really was simple. It took a good month to do all of this, but we worked at a slower pace than the fast-paced season. When we finished cleaning everything, we lugged it down into the storage area. We made sure to mark everything so we knew where to bring it back at the start of the next season (a process that for some reason failed when we began setting up for the next season). We did a great job in cleaning, and I learned about the products that clean—so much so, that I decided to take a few cleaning products home with me to freshen up my bathroom.

The end of the season in September contains the same feeling and scent as the beginning of the football season. Temperatures begin to drop, giving the air that crisp feel, and the air jumps in sparkles, exciting your step; at least this was true for me. In regards to football, the Cleveland Browns began their first season in three years. After three Brownless years, the fabulous orange helmets ran on to the field. For the past three years, Sundays meant nothing more or less than any other day—there was no significance. While many threw on their lazy clothes and crowded around a bowl of nachos and salsa on Sundays, I went about my business, living my life and avoiding the NFL. I call this the Browns Factor. I never really missed the NFL; in fact, the lack of the Browns was quite liberating—not having to worry on Sundays; not having to wake on Monday and get struck with that sudden surge of disappointment; I really missed nothing about it. But now, the Browns were back—the new Browns. Art Modell was gone, and this began a new era. An era of success. An era of a Super Bowl appearance! Perhaps I just got all caught up in the excitement and return of the Browns, but for the next few years I regressed to keeping my Sundays open so that I could watch the Browns. On the contrary, during the Browns absence, my enthusiasm for sports crashed like a bloody drunken driver light-pole crash—smash. The loss of the Browns not only hurt my passion for football, but it also tore away at my love for sports in general. Little by little, my vivacious love for sports had faded. The lack of football allowed me to spend time finding interest in other facets of life. By the time the Browns rolled back around, my interest lie elsewhere. Fitting the Browns back into my schedule of "must-do's" proved difficult. My mind often wandered during games. As a youngster, I made sure to see each and every play. Now, with the new Browns, if I missed a play here or there, it made no difference. Similarly, after a loss, when I awoke on Monday, I felt no lingering pain. I was able to go about my day. Now, the games still excited me; it was just a different excitement. Again, studying the Browns Factor leads me to believe that the loss of the Browns probably had something to do with my lack of interest in sports; however, smothered by an overwhelming immersion of sports, I still charge the bulk of the blame to my horrific experience of working in baseball.

In the end, like the beginning of the football season, where all the guys gather together with beer and pretzels to watch the first game, the beginning of the baseball off-season ignites a stimulating vibe that provides the people who work in baseball with an opportunity to revitalize their strengths and mentality, allowing them to believe they can engage in another season of early mornings, intense days and late nights.

PART III

14 FUZZY THE BEAR?

"Fuzzy the Cougar!" exclaimed my coworker. She was introducing the furry mascot from the Southtown Guitars.

With the pounding of the Village People's YMCA, Fuzzy revealed himself from one of the doorways and ran across the gym. He ran up into the gym bleachers where the students sat. Fuzzy jumped back down onto the gym floor and began running full speed toward some bowling pins that the physical education teacher had painstakingly set up for the next gym class. Fuzzy exploded into a Pete Rose slide and hit the pins head first. Strike! The students laughed and cheered, and I looked up through the mesh eyes on Fuzzy's head. I was Fuzzy. I clapped my hands together and waved to the crowd of junior high students. I performed a couple more dance steps and slid down onto my knees for a finale.

During the off season, I traveled to local schools as Fuzzy the Cougar. We promoted the Southtown Guitars Reading Program. Students read so many books and received Guitars tickets in return. The school could make a whole event of it if they wanted. Somehow, I agreed to play the part of Fuzzy the Cougar, mascot of the Southtown Guitars—don't ask. Laura, my coworker, did all the talking, while I played the cougar. We traveled all around the state. At first, the whole Fuzzy thing was great fun. I enjoyed fooling around and acting like a comic behind the disguise of a cougar. But as time passed, the steaming hot interiors of Fuzzy became unbearable. After time, the insides of Fuzzy stunk of mildewed sweat, hence I began to smell as such. Once the Guitars staff caught wind of how great a promotional tactic Fuzzy was, they were signing me up to go all over the place, often without another staff member there to act as an Fuzzy bodyguard. Fuzzy needed a guard. Without the help of another staff member, Fuzzy could come under great abuse.

So, the assembly at the junior high ended, and I made one last run around the gym. I charged up the bleachers, and, on my way back down the stands, a girl grabbed onto my hand. The Velcro around the hand tore off, and I stumbled onto the gym floor with no hand. I quickly pulled my hand into the cougar's skin and pretended that my hand had actually been ripped off my arm. I gyrated around the floor and then stopped. Laura ran over and helped me up, and she assisted me off the gym floor, handless.

I walked down the hallway of the school with kids shouting, "Bye bear," or "I love you monkey." It was hard to tell that Fuzzy was a cougar.

After our stay at the Middle of Nowhere Junior High, we drove to the Fucking Middle of Nowhere Elementary School. Sometimes we had two or three appearances in a row. This made it difficult for the sweaty Fuzzy. Do I travel as Fuzzy, squished in the front seat of a car? Do I change back to a human and change the sweaty clothes, only to sweatify another pair of clothes at the next performance? I never got this answer right. Whichever approach I took was misery. On this day, the next school was right down the street, so I suffered the claustrophobia of being scrunched in the front seat of Laura's car as Fuzzy.

At each Fuzzy appearance, I found that kid who could not let Fuzzy go. Sometimes, it was a nice innocent little girl who just wanted to hug Fuzzy and show him around.

Other times, it was some brat-ass kid who just wanted to beat the hell out of Fuzzy. At this performance, there was some fifth grader with a moustache who just wanted to kick Fuzzy in the balls. Every chance he got he tried to kick me in the balls. Sometimes, Laura caught him and told him, "Fuzzy doesn't like that. It hurts him." But, no matter; the kid struggled in fury to get at me. With his legs swinging, he fought off my bodyguard and hit me square in the balls. For refuge, I ducked into the restroom and took a breather. I took my Fuzzy head off and bent over the sink, spitting Fuzzy hairs into the kiddy sink. The kid followed me in and saw me without my head. He paused for a second and stared. I slowly opened my eyes real wide. His eyes slowly bulged from his mustachioed head, and he began to cry and ran out. Ha! Ha! I got that kid. I strapped the head back on and walked out of the restroom feeling good. When I got out, the kid was waiting. He pulled his arm back and smashed me right in the face, spinning my head around. I was not hurt, but I took this time to lie on the floor. All of a sudden, a bunch of kids jumped on top of me. I was suffocating. I thought I might die as Fuzzy. I could hear the ball-kicking kid screaming that I was a man and not a bear. With kids plowing into me and landing cannonballs on my furry belly, I laid staring at the ceiling. What the fuck am I doing? What's going on here? Am I really here, lying on a school floor? Oof!—a kid landed an elbow in my sternum. Finally, Laura came to the rescue.

"Come on Fuzzy. Let's go to Mrs. Garman's room," Laura said.

"Laura, I'm done. I gotta get out of here," I whispered.

"C'mon, one more room."

"Laura, I'm dying."

Laura led me by my arm to Mrs. Garman's room. Her class was not in there yet, and Laura said we should wait. I decided to go in and surprise Mrs. Garman. I snuck up behind her and scared her. Unfortunately, she held a cup of coffee in her hand, and it splashed up on her clothes. I immediately took my head off and apologized. She insisted that it was all right, but I felt like an ass. The class filed in and Laura and I did our thing.

Usually, I ran around the room, rubbing kids' heads or acting like a clown. Sometimes I sat on a small kid and pretended not to know. Other times I messed with the teachers—the kids loved that one. I tried many things to get the kids interested, and to keep my interest. Eventually, I slowed down, and Laura made the introductions. She explained the reading program and passed out prizes to kids who got trivia questions correct. Finally, Laura read a short book to the class. I have to say, I did like the classroom setting. I enjoyed making the kids laugh and getting them excited about reading.

We finally ended our appearance and started to leave. We pushed our way through a crowd of kids. All of a sudden, I came to an opening where the ball-kicker kid stood. He was waiting for me. I proceeded forward and stepped on the kid's foot really hard before he could lift it up to kick me. I walked away leaving him screaming that I stepped on his foot.

We left the building and the backwoods of nowhere in the rearview mirror. The long trips back to Southtown gave me time to reflect on my job and life. As the Fuzzy appearances continued, my reflections became more depressing. Plus, since the end of the season, the companionship between Butch and me deteriorated because of our different off-season jobs. During the off season, Butch sold advertising and promotions. This gave us little time to talk at work, which translated into less time outside of work. I started to feel alone in my Southtown world, and my job didn't help.

Laura and I visited many schools for the reading program—187 to be exact. We traveled all throughout the region, encompassing hundreds of square miles. We drove out to regions of the United States where I never thought there'd be any necessity for a school. We visited children who never saw buildings higher than three stories. We passed historic monuments, such as Civil War memorials commemorating southern heroes like Jefferson Davis. With each trip came a different school and experience.

In addition, the Fuzzy costume acted as an instant dehydration device. My hairy casing forced sweat to flow from my pores like floodwaters, causing me to lose what seemed like gallons of body liquid. At each chance, I asked Laura to stop for something to drink. Most all of the places we stopped were secluded gas stations. In these backwoods regions of nowhere, the gas stations served home cooked fried foods. Some of the places even had slabs of some dried meat hanging from the ceiling, not sure what that was all about.

"Excuse me." I asked the attendant behind the counter.
"Yes, honey?"
"What are those things hanging there?"
"Oh," she laughed a little, "that's cured ham, honey."
"Oh."

I have to admit, it was interesting traveling through the backwoods of the southern culture. We drank sweet tea and ate okra at Meat 'n Three's, and most of this became natural to me.

At the same time, I could not get my mind off of one thing. Many teachers at the schools we visited were young and beautiful. I always wanted to ask one of them out on a date, but it was hard enough to get a date with a teacher during school hours, let alone when wearing a fucking cougar costume. I never knew quite how to go about asking these teachers out, so I didn't. Instead, I accepted the humiliation in front of girls I would rather be dating. Sure, they laughed at my silly antics, but it was not really the communication I wanted.

Laura and I were back out on the road. We entered an older looking elementary school. It wasn't a bad gig. One little girl loved me. Or should I say, she loved Fuzzy. She looked up to me...er...him. I mean, she really looked up to me. On our stroll down the little halls, she would periodically look up at me with the most preciously childlike look. I mean, she was a child. She constantly wanted to make sure I was with her. She held my hairy hand tight as she led me around her school. This was another out-of-the-way school.

Initially, I held her hand and followed, to humor her, but eventually, as I had time to think, the whole scene began to sadden me. This little girl loved me like she did her teddy bear. She saw true loyalty and trust in me. Who knows, perhaps her family life was far from perfect. Perhaps her parents were divorced. Perhaps her parents were together but fought constantly. Perhaps she was ignored at home. Or, heck, perhaps she had the perfect family at home, but just loved having a furry friend. Whatever the case, she looked up to me. Me, a furry, mildewed man. An unshaven man. An overweight man. A depressed and sweaty man. A man who cursed under his breath with each Fuzzy appearance. A man lost with no idea about the future.

I felt bad for little Becca. In all honesty, her wellbeing placed nowhere in my top interests. My number one interest, of course, was getting out of this rancid costume. If I could only scratch those itchy spots that migrated over my cougar-covered body like nomadic annoyances.

Here she was holding my hand with naïve love, and all I could do was to think of her teacher, whose blouse hung a bit low, allowing bra visibility. I'd seen bras in the store before, and they did nothing to arouse my caveman tendencies. But, a bra hiding behind a blouse that loosely clung to a woman's body was another thing. Becca's teacher's neck blossomed bare from her very feminine collarbones. Her bra made a very lazy effort to play Puritan police, as much of her chest breathed fresh, exposed to the school air, scented with crayon. Becca's teacher's skirt hung just below the knee but danced freely with each step. Her heeled shoes caused a sexual stretch in her calf that should have excited even the 5th graders.

"Fuzzy!" Becca shouted, shaking me from my dreamy state. "You need to pay attention," Becca said innocently, patting my furry hand like a kitten.

Becca guided me through the halls to the next room.

"This is where you're going next. I have to leave, so don't be afraid. I'll be back," Becca spoke like a loving parent. Her true compassion almost made me cry.

Laura stood waiting for me outside the door and asked, "Where ya been Fuzzy? They're waiting for us."

I shrugged.

"I'll go in and prep 'em, and I'll signal when to come in."

I nodded.

While Laura prepped the class inside, a little boy came walking down the hall. I noticed him as he first turned the corner. It took him a few seconds to reach me, but his eyes never left my face. His intense eyes watched me like a hawk, as if the cougar was his prey. I waved when he was close. Like a lightning bolt, he threw a punch into my hip. It startled me, but my boney hip must have hurt his knuckles. He ran crying, "The bear hurt me!"

Scared, I didn't want to wait for Laura to finish. I busted through the door in the middle of her spiel.

"I wasn't finished yet, Fuzzy."

I raced around the room like a clown, patting kids' heads and knocking books onto the floor. Kids giggled.

"And here's Fuzzy." Laura had no other move than to announce me.

I sat on the teacher's desk and used her head as an armrest. This got a big laugh. The teacher put up with it. She was a bit older and wore a bee's nest. It was comfy under my elbow. I picked up a book and opened it upside down and pretended to read.

"It's upside down," the class yelled, laughing all the while.

"Okay, Fuzzy. Why don't you take a seat, and I'll read the book," Laura said somewhat motherly.

I sat on the rug in the corner, and all of the kids gathered around me. Some forced their way to sit by me so they could pet me as Laura read. Some whispered, "I love you," during the reading, and I just patted them on the head.

When I wore my own flesh, I commanded little respect or interest. I was quite invisible outside the costume. In disguise, playing a cougar, I was quite popular. It was sometimes a nice distraction from reality. The innocent attention of the kids kept me upbeat much of the time, even if I had no chance with their teachers.

At the same time, I continued feeling the weight of humiliation. I continued my battles against little punk-ass motherfuckers who wanted to beat my balls into oblivion. I continued jumping around like a silly fuck and listening to comments like, "Oh, you're just Fuzzy. Where is the Guitars rep?" All of this took its toll on me so that by winter I had had enough. Of course, I was still a young inexperienced loyal employee of the Southtown Guitars. My belief was that this was my job and I had to do my best at it. So, I continued my Fuzzy performances. I continued to pack two extra pairs of clothes for work. I continued to buy obscene amounts of bottled water. I was Fuzzy, and this was the way it was. Period.

BIT 15: SEE YOU BUTCH

I went home for Christmas that winter. Butch asked for a ride to see his brother who lived around the Akron area. So Butch and I drove up to Akron, and we exchanged many of the same stories (I was doing little of the storytelling). While up in Akron, Butch called me several times to get together, but I really didn't want to be reminded of my job while on break. I declined his offers to get together for the College Bowl games, and I think he felt disappointed in my refusal. I felt secure and at ease in the house of my youth. I rested on the couch and flipped on the television without ever being reminded of the Guitars. The mad rush of Christmas comforted me like a blanket, and I loved every moment of it. All of this kept my mind busy with little time for wandering.

In any case, I told everyone that I was the mascot for a minor league team in Southtown. Some people laughed and thought it was great, while others seemed confused and unsatisfied with my occupation. I understood all the reactions I got. I was not even really happy with my job, and I'm sure some people could sense it. But, like my work with Hitler, I continued to persevere and put myself through agony. Was the job all that bad? I was working, getting paid. In fact, the thought of looking for another job never crossed my mind. Nobody else was looking for a job. Thinking back, I compare the whole experience to high school—you sit in blank, medicinal classrooms for four years, not because you like it, rather it's just what you do. I never thought of leaving the Guitars just like I never thought of leaving high school. Instead, I robotically woke up early every day and worked the best I could.

My disillusionment with work increased with the arrival of two new Guitars employees, Todd and Wally. Wally shared my exact birthday, and Todd was a few months younger. These two guys were in group sales. They immediately surpassed me on the staff. Even though we were the same age, I was inferior, and I felt it. The worst was when they booked me for a Fuzzy appearance. If anything, I thought, I should be booking them. While my disappointment continued, my grudges didn't last. The more I got to know these two, the better I felt about them. We spent a lot of time watching ESPN and going out to the local hangs. We found a lot to joke about, and the three of use became good friends—guys my age to hang out with. As I became closer to Todd and Wally, Butch and I grew further apart.

Though we began to spend less time together, Butch and I still maintained our unspoken agreement of trust at work. Our last real hurrah came during a season ticket holders' party in January. Butch and I cooked the food for the event on a charcoal grill in the concourse, while everyone else schmoozed upstairs in the restaurant. Butch and I took the job with pleasure. We got to hang out while everybody else wore his prettiest collar. We decided to borrow some of the leftover beer from the season that sat chilling in the vending cooler. There we stood, drinking beer and telling stories. When it was just the two of us, we reverted back to the old days. We cooked our food and sent it upstairs. Butch ran upstairs to check on some of his clients, and I stayed downstairs sipping my beer. It was a relaxing night at the grill, until...Butch came down and told me that Al wanted me to suit up in the cougar outfit and shake hands upstairs.

"Really?" I asked.
"Yeah, man."
"I'm drunk."

Butch laughed, "Fuck it Fuz. You got a restless crowd up there."

I ran upstairs into the office and slipped on the mildewed mess of hair. I stumbled into the elevator and busted into the restaurant. I danced around the restaurant, shaking hands and rubbing beer-bellied old men's bald heads. I spanked old ladies and even gave Al a bear hug. The whole place loved it, and they never knew that I was smashed. I even spoke a few words even though Fuzzy was not supposed to talk. I considered doing this drunk all the time, if only schools served beer.

16 SEASON TWO ROLLS AROUND WITHOUT A BANG

The new season approached and reunited Butch and me. We needed to organize the concessions and get the stadium ready for the hotdog-hungry people. The process of readying the stands for the new season was identical to cleaning the stands at the end of the previous season, only backwards. Also, at the end of the season, the cool fall weather felt good, a nice change to the unbearable summer heat. Cleaning the stands in the cold of early spring was not as welcoming. Our hands froze from the soapy water we cleaned with; accidentally slamming a hammer on a frozen finger caused unfathomable pain. The sharp edges of the many metal devices used in concessions sliced our hands relentlessly. We dropped heavy hotdog warmers on our feet constantly. We basically knocked the shit out of ourselves in order to get the stadium ready for our next season of bludgeoning.

The more we worked the fewer questions we asked—we became mindless robots, addicted to laboring for nothing. Today, I find it difficult to completely condemn the job; if anything, I arrived in Southtown without the important knowledge of work and responsibility. The backbreaking agony of concessions and the fear of Al provided me with the initial push needed for me to start myself down the road of understanding responsibility. Also, the constant unhappiness with the work persuaded me to look for more in life. At the same time, I found the job itself complete misery.

For a moment, I saw the light at the start of the new season. The Guitars hired new interns, and I dumped Fuzzy onto them. Al assigned several of the interns to assist at Hitler. Help... I'll have real help! Help that I could trust. Will this season be easier? How could it not be?

We worked every day of the week during the month leading up to the new season, cleaning and fixing the stadium. This really upset me. I had very little free time. I woke up early one Sunday morning so I could go to church; I needed a pleasant time to myself, away from the stadium. The Sunday before the home opener, my dad called me. I spoke to him while lying in bed. We talked about my job, and I assured him that it was fine.

"What are you doing, Anton?" he asked. He knew I could do better.

"What?" This was always my response to my dad when I knew he was right but I was embarrassed to admit it.

"What do you mean 'what'? I know you can do more."

I knew he was right, but I just sat on the phone in silence. We said our goodbyes, and I sat back and thought for a moment. What was I doing? I was twenty-four years old, and I still felt too young to make a career decision. Will the Guitars be my career? Can I make a career in baseball? I thought about all the experiences I had with the Guitars—pretty silly lifestyle, but it built character and responsibility. Still, I always found it hard to glance up into the stands where people enjoyed a beer, friends and a game, sitting in the Saturday afternoon sun with a sense of peace. How many summers can I go on watching people enjoy baseball? I didn't enjoy any of the games. My mind wandered and concentrated on depressed visions. I even thought of the staff. I thought about a few days earlier when Butch and I took Partner out for lunch to a Chinese restaurant. Earlier that day, Partner lost the keys to the four-wheeler that the grounds crew used to transport dirt and tools. He repeatedly said, "I...I...I...gotta find those keys, man."

While eating our Chinese buffet of unidentified dishes, Butch and I pressed the key situation.

"You lost the keys, Partner." Butch said in a stern voice.

"No, man. I...did...not...man." he said this last sentence one word at a time, concentrating on the pronunciation.

"Al's gonna be pissed, Partner." Butch said, trying his best to stir panic in Partner.

"I know. I know, man."

We ate more, and Partner spoke of the keys again. Finally, Butch asked, "Partner, is it true you're Mel Belle's twin?"

"It's true, man. It's true."

Butch and I looked at each other and smiled. Butch added, "You look nothing alike."

"It ain't true, man. It ain't true."

"You're not twins?" I jokingly asked.

"Yes...we...are, man." Again, Partner spoke in a slowed pace, pronouncing each word as if it were its own entity.

We laughed, and Partner started on the keys again.

I shook my brain away from my daydreaming of Partner and the keys, and I refocused my thoughts to the question at hand, What was I doing? Were silly moments like the one with Partner enough to keep me working in baseball—is that a career? Baseball, concessions and Fuzzy were all that I knew. I knew the process behind all of them. I knew my schedule. I was learning some of the Reading Club selling points. Did I just want to scrap all that I knew in baseball and start from scratch somewhere else? Baseball had become too natural for me to truly assess it, but I did know I had a deep, internal aggravation about the idea of a career in baseball.

It seemed like everyone enjoyed working at the stadium and hanging out with each other. I, on the other hand, began to hate the stadium and everything that went into it.

I hated the constant smell of soured milk that lingered by the dumpster. I hated the fear that constantly buzzed about my head. I began walking away from conversations centering on sports. Anybody questioning me about my opinion on what player ran the best on frozen turf received a contorted smirk and shrugged shoulders, accompanied by complete silence. Who cared about this player's reoccurring groin pull or that team's success rate on Monday night football after a bye week? These questions seemed mere distractions to real problems. I developed an almost unhealthy cynicism to sports. I conjured the conclusion that the sports world manifested pointless dilemmas in order to make headlines or attract fans. There was all too much—too much "sports." I felt over-sported, and I wanted no more of it. All this sports talk was useless, irritatingly useless!

For the first time, I began thinking of leaving. But these were short-lived thoughts. Then, something happened that pressured me into staying with the Guitars.

On the eve of the season opener, Todd, Wally, and I decided to have a feast. We thought that this night would be our last night of freedom for months. Before we left, I decided to call my mom to say hello, because I knew I wouldn't talk to her during the first home stand. My grandmother answered the phone and told me that my father had been taken to the hospital, and my mom went to go see him. My grandmother told me that it was pretty serious. Stunned, I slowly walked out to my car in a half daze. Todd and Wally asked me if I was going to meet them at the restaurant, and I said yes. But I was not going to meet them at the restaurant. I drove home with horrible visions racing through my head. I made it to my apartment and walked directly to my bedroom. I sat back on the bed and stared at the ceiling. My roommate Ricki came in and told me that he was getting pizza and wondered if I wanted any. I told him no thanks and continued my staring. About an hour later, my mom called me and told me that my father had a stroke and was not in very good condition. We stayed on the phone for a while, exchanging comments of disbelief. Nothing was really said. She told me to come home.

The next morning, I woke early for the home opener and got into work. I did not know what I was going to do. I walked around the office a little, and then I entered Al's office and began to cry. I told him my situation, and he called the airlines and bought me a plane ticket. I told him that I was sorry because I was leaving him during the home opener.

"Nah," he gave me a look that told me my comment was ridiculous, "some things are more important than baseball." I never thought I would ever hear this guy say something like that, but I realized then that there was some rationality within the walls of Al's head. However, that really didn't matter to me now. The man understood my predicament, and he helped me out. I told him that I would get him started at the grill before I left, and he told me that he could get Wally to do it. Together we found Butch and Wally and walked to Hitler. Al had just demanded some new colorful picnic signs be posted that labeled where each picnic was. I pointed one out to him that read, "Black Picnic Area." He laughed and agreed that the sign needed to be changed. I gave Wally some quick pointers about cooking time, the pilot light, and all the other nonsensical essentials involving Hitler. Butch and I took a walk to the warehouse to grab some gloves for Wally. While in the warehouse, Butch offered me the money in his pocket.

"No, thanks," I said.

"Take it. You might need it. Do you have any cash on you?"

"No, but I'll just get some."

"Take it. I want to do this for you."

"Thank you." I took the money. I smiled and left the stadium.

Originally, I told Al that I was going to pack some things and come back and help before I had to catch my plane, but, while I was out, I just wanted to drive around. I knew my father would appreciate me getting my car washed, so I did. I got to the airport a couple hours early and read a book. I think I was too stunned to cry.

I flew home, and some friends picked me up at the airport. They drove me home and helped to lighten the mood a bit. But, when I opened the door to my house, I began crying in whosever arms I fell into. From one person to the next, I cried in their hugs of pain and love. That evening, my two brothers and I sprawled out wherever we could in my mom's room. The sound of my father's voice saying, "What are you doing" kept going through my head. The four of us just lay there, comforting each other. My dad was dead.

I stayed at home for about a week. Finally, my roommate, Ricki, called me to see how things were going. I had moved in with Ricki after being kicked out of my first apartment, which my cousin found for me. Ricki was a stellar roommate, and we enjoyed rooting for the Indians through the play-offs. Ricki told me that Al thought that I wasn't going to return. Al thought that I would quit the Guitars and stay at home. This angered me for some reason. I became determined to prove myself. I walked upstairs to where my mom was lying down and told her that I thought I should be going back to Southtown. She told me that I had my own life to live and that I should do whatever I thought would be best. My older brother and I both flew out the same day, leaving my mom and younger brother alone.

When I showed up for work, I think I surprised everyone. The entire staff told me that they were sorry about my father, but I refused to let any pain show. I smiled and thanked them. I was prepared to show everyone that I was strong, and I could go on.

In one case, a client of one of our salesmen stood in the lobby. I walked in, dirty from my work. The salesman pointed me out and told the client that I was the one whose father had just died. The man walked over and put his hand on the employee right next to me and gave his condolences. Apparently, the man thought that the salesman pointed at the guy next to me. The client walked away with a smile.

The greatest part upon returning was the matching of Wally and me at Hitler. Wally's dad had died several years earlier in a fire. Wally helped me a lot by talking to me about a subject I was deathly afraid of. He also gave good advice. He told me that his dad always saved his money and lived his life very conservatively. Wally said that all of a sudden, his dad was dead, and his dad never really allowed himself to have fun in his life. Because of this, Wally decided to live his life in the opposite manner. The conversation helped us grow closer—a needed element in the cooperation of running Hitler. I took Wally's advice to heart, and began reevaluating my own life, searching for ways to take full advantage of life.

17 GRILLBILLIES

The grill ran smoothly with Wally and me at the helm. Hitler still battled us all the way, but, between the two of us, we managed with only a few headaches and burns. Wally possessed a confidence that laughed in the face of trouble, and his attitude rubbed off onto me. Also, the fact that we could rely on each other helped me to relax and not get so uptight. Our confidence ballooned to the point where we hunted down new challenges. About midway through the season, Wally and I spotted a great dare. We had a Saturday sellout approaching with an early Sunday game. There were going to be thousands of little reading program kids at the Sunday game, all of whom were to receive a free hotdog. This meant that Wally and I had to start cooking early—6 a.m. early. We figured that we would get finished with everything around 1 a.m. on Saturday, and we also figured that going home to sleep would be a waste of time. We decided to spend the night at the stadium, playing video games on the restaurant television. This all made perfect sense to us at the time.

On Saturday, we finished around 1 a.m. and told Al that we were staying overnight. "Oh, yeah," he suspiciously smiled with an air of skepticism, but he let us go our way. Wally and I set up the video game in the restaurant, and, once we had that set to go, we turned our taste buds toward the beer taps behind the bar. We filled up a pitcher and began playing. Time moved slowly as we filled pitcher after pitcher and played game after game. By 2:30 a.m., we were already looking for something new to do, but now we had less sense than before. We were drunk. The hot tub! Yes! The hot tub! We decided to take a dip in the stadium hot tub, a facility reserved for groups. We filled up a couple pitchers of beer and ran our intoxicated bodies through the concourse to the hot tub, leaving a trail of spilt beer as we ran. We turned the bubbles on and relaxed in the quiet Southtown night.

"That would have sucked to drive home and go to bed," I slurred.

"No joke," Wally laughed his staple response.

"Let's see, we got 6,000 dogs to cook first for the little bastards."

"Fuck, yeah," Wally laughed.

"And then, we got another 6,000 for the picnics and stands to start things off."

"Yeah. It won't be bad. Today...or I guess...yesterday we had to cook for a lot more than that."

"Yeah. Those picnics were ridiculous."

"No, joke. That was so funny today when you started smashing Hitler," he said.

"Well the fucker wouldn't quit fuckin' up!"

Wally continued to laugh, "Did you see the dents you put in that bastard?"

"Ahh, shit. I don't give a fuck."

There was a pause while we reflected on the day. Then Wally spoke up, "Hey, whatdya think of Irene?"

"I think she's a prissy whore."

"Why do you say that?"

"I don't know. I just wanted to say that." I didn't really like Irene. She was a new intern. She was good looking, but she thought a little too much of herself. She had recently broken off an engagement with her fiancé. I think she enjoyed bonking the young men on the staff a little too much.

Sweaty Mascots start Grease Fires

"Remember the trip down the Ocoee River?" Wally reflected.

"That was so hilarious." A few weeks back, the Guitars collected a bunch of us together and bused us to the Ocoee River for some whitewater rafting. About a dozen of us went, including Irene. We all drank ourselves to death during the bus ride. While we raged through the demonic waters, Wally bounced overboard—too drunk, I presume. After our river adventure, we made our way to a bar. All the while, Irene drank herself into oblivion.

"Remember when Irene had her face in Dom's lap," Wally said in between laughs. "His pants were undone!"

"I know!"

"Her face was right in his underwear!"

"Wet underwear!" I laughed.

"Oh yeah! He was pourin' beer on his own crotch!"

"And she was lickin' it up! Whore, I tell ya. Whore!"

Then, from nowhere, Wally bluntly said, "Carter fucked her last week." He was referring to one of the many new interns.

I was surprised. "Really? When?"

"After we had gone swimming at our apartment complex."

"No shit? Shit."

"I guess he poked her in the butt."

"Really." All this was news to me.

"Yeah. She asked him to."

An explosion of laughter stopped the conversation for a moment. Wally spilled his beer in the hot tub. We laughed more, and I filled him up with my pitcher, dripping most of the beer into the tub.

Wally continued, "A couple days before, Reid fucked her in the ass."

"What?" I had been blind. I had not spotted any of this fucking. Reid was another one of the interns who we had started to hang out with.

"Yeah," Wally laughed, "when he pulled out his dick, there was a piece of corn on it, and she licked it off."

I bellowed out an enormous call for humanity, "Oh c'mon!"

We erupted into loud hoots and hollers. We shouted whatever ridiculous comment came to our mind. After a short lull, Wally suggested a most devilish proposal.

"You wanna go to a whorehouse?" Wally blurted from nowhere again.

"You serious?" I asked, hoping it was his thoughts about Irene and not the fact that he was sitting in a hot tub with me that inspired him to say this.

"Yeah."

"You know where one is?"

"Yeah, let's go."

I was a little unsure of the whorehouse. I had never been to one, and I didn't really want to start going on this night. The last time I got myself into one of these situations, I caught myself staring at a midget in the dark neighborhoods behind the stadium. However, Wally insisted, and I bounced the idea around in my dizzy head. I had never had sex with a girl I liked, let alone a prostitute.

"Alright. Let's go." I decided to go along with Wally's suggestion. Maybe it was the beer, or maybe it was peer pressure. Or, still yet, maybe I just wanted to go with the flow and not worry about it. Whatever it was, we went. We jumped out of the beer-tainted tub and ran back upstairs. We hopped into Wally's car and headed toward the whorehouse. I still don't know where this place is in Southtown. I was so drunk during the drive that my vision was warped by the stream of streetlights that we passed. To me, it was just a giggle away. We pulled up to the place, and Wally started to get out of the car. I sat in the car, oblivious to the fact that we had arrived. Wally shouted me out of my daze, and together we walked in. I remember being greeted by an Asian lady of about 40. Another girl stepped out from behind a curtain. She was smashingly ugly and about 35 years. I think I even remember Marvin Gaye's "Let's Get it On" playing in the background as the 35-year old relaxed on the door frame. I remember a lot of greens, oranges and reds—the carpet, the lighting, and the television worked together to created this imagery. The Asian girl held out her hand as if to introduce the girl.

"Who wants to go first?" I am not sure where this voice came from, but I know these words were spoken.

We both paused. I paused because I was uncertain that I wanted to do this. Even in my state, I thought, "Do I want this on my credit card?" Wally stepped past me and walked behind the curtain with the old lady. I looked back at the Asian lady, but she was gone. The television was on in the lobby, playing some late night movie. I took a seat on the couch nearby and waited for something to happen. Was I going to go through with it? Nobody was around. It was just me sitting on a couch in front of a television. I could have been home and the setting would have been the same. A few minutes passed before another girl stepped out from behind the curtain with another guy. She showed him out, and then she took a seat across from me. She was younger, younger than me.

"Hi," I decided to break the silence.

She responded with a shy "hi" and a smile.

"How old are you?" Despite my hard buzz, I managed to focus a train of thought, and I became quite curious about the girl.

"Eighteen." There was a pause while I nodded my head, and then, "I just graduated from high school."

"Oh." Another pause. I felt a little uncomfortable, but I didn't know what else to do.

"You, ahh, been doing this long?"

"About two months."

"Great. Great." I didn't know what other response to offer, so I just nodded and offered another uninspiring "Great."

We turned to the television for a bit and watched an awful scene from an awful movie. I don't remember anything about it other than a truck roared through several lanes of traffic. I turned back toward her.

"You like working here?"

"It's alright."

"Great." The whole time I wondered if I should ask her to go to the back room. Is that what she was waiting for? Maybe she just wanted a break from the fucking. Maybe she just wanted to sit and talk to a stranger instead of fuck him. I bored her some by telling her I worked for the Guitars, and, soon after, Wally came from the curtain, wearing a straight face—an intentional straight face during an awkward moment. He paid with his credit card, and I said bye to the girl. As we walked out, he started laughing and said, "Geez, you're fast! Speedy Gonzalez!" He continued this as we walked toward the door and out. "Did you even do anything?" Just then, a police cruiser sped up to the door. Wally screamed, "The cops!" Wally took off running, and I followed. When I was sitting, I felt fine, but I could feel the alcohol creep up my throat when I ran. Wally charged up a wall of tires, and I followed (apparently, the whorehouse sat right next to a car garage, this particular car garage had assembled a wall of tires high enough to challenge the most skilled rock climber). I staggered up the wobbling structure of synthetic rubber. At the top of this wall of tires was a fence. Wally scaled it with martial arts-like bullet-time skills. I followed, scraping my side. I collapsed on the other side of the fence and caught up to Wally. We ran through neighborhood streets and backyards. And after a lengthy run, we came to Wally's car, accompanied by a jubilant laughter.

"Fuck, how'd your car get here?" I asked out of breath.

"This is where we parked."

"I'm glad you remembered."

We sped off down the street, passing the police cruiser in front of the whorehouse.

"Damn, that was close," Wally huffed.

We made it back to the stadium and ran back to the hot tub. Wally asked me about my whorehouse experience. He noticed the girl I was talking too, and he admitted that she was much better looking than his girl. Out of pride and

Sweaty Mascots start Grease Fires

peer pressure, I told him that I had just gotten a hand job. He fucked his girl for $80.

"The girl started out kissing my chest and shit," Wally said. "Fuck that. I just wanted to fuck." He started laughing again and chirped, "Speedy Gonzalez! I don't understand. How'd you do it so fast? What, did she stroke you off as you walked to the back room?" Wally continued to laugh, and I laughed in reaction, as a sort of defense mechanism.

We wobbled up to the stadium and sipped miserably at some beers. It was 4:50 a.m. We had to start cooking hotdogs in almost an hour. In order to gain our second wind, Wally decided to cook some eggs and bacon for us. I disintegrated into a couch and closed my eyes.

The next thing I knew, Kurt the restaurant guy was in my face, yelling, "Hakos. Hakos. What's up?"

I shook my head and thought for a second. I felt completely disoriented. "What's going on?" Suddenly it hit me. "What time is it?" I asked with a shock of fear ripping away my heart.

"6:30," Kurt answered.

"Fuck!" We were late. We had passed out. We should have started cooking at 6 a.m. if we wanted to get the 6,000 hot dogs for the kiddies done in time. I saw Wally slumped in the couch across from me. "Wally, Wally!" I woke Wally. He slowly rose from his couch and dumped the empty plate of eggs and bacon.

"What's going on?" He asked.

"It's 6:30! We're late!" A grin grew on Wally's face.

Wally erupted into a nonstop laugh and said, "We're fucked!"

Those words felt like a spear being slowly pulled from my gut, removing some innards with it, causing a mess of mixed body organs to crumble within me.

The next thing I knew, I was racking hotdogs faster than I ever had. I don't even know how I got down to the grill, but there I was, racking dogs. Opposite me was

Wally, laughing, "We're fucked, we're fucked." He sounded possessed, unable to stop giggling.

"Shut the fuck up, Wally!" I didn't want to hear the truth that we were fucked. But Wally continued to laugh.

"We're fucked."

I desperately tried to focus on the task at hand. Is there anything I'm forgetting? Do I have the right number of cases ready for cooking? My brain quickly ran through a list of grill to-do's. But it was difficult to think. Each thought struggled its way through a thick webbing of dead brain cells. I glanced up at Hitler's thermometer and noticed that it read nowhere near the needed 400 degrees. I lifted open the lid and found that all the burners were out.

"We're fucked," Wally continued hysterically.

"I gotta re-light the pilot light."

"Oh, shit, we can't have any problems with the grill today," Wally laughed.

I was concentrating too hard to answer. Plus, I felt too scared to even listen to Wally. I grabbed the lighter and knelt down by the front pilot light. But the pilot light wasn't the only thing out—the lighter was out of lighter fluid. I clicked and clicked the damn thing in hopes of igniting a flame, but it was useless. Can I call on the radio? No. Al would realize there was a problem. I searched my brain, attempting to think if we had another lighter. Slowly my neurotransmitters shot attempted messages throughout my brain. My eyes helped my brain by fluttering back and forth. My mouth degenerated into a biting frenzy, nibbling on my inner cheeks. There had to be an answer. Yes. The lighter that fell behind the pizza oven last year. I gave up on reaching for the lighter last year because I thought it lost forever. Now, in this time of need, I knew that I could rescue the lost lighter. I ran into the cooler room and flopped down on my belly to look under the mammoth pizza oven. While the front of my shirt soaked up year-old grease, I spotted the savior. I looked around for a broom or anything that could reach. The brooms were too short.

Sweaty Mascots start Grease Fires

"What can I use?" I looked at the pizza oven and noticed a dangling metal lining that ran the length of the oven. I muscled it off and was about to fish around for the lighter when Butch appeared.

"How's things going down here?"

"I got no lighter."

Butch reached in his pocket, "Here, use this one."

I shook my head of its stupidity and grabbed Butch's lighter. I lit the pilot light, but the morning breeze was too much. Fuck. I built another barrier around the pilot lights in order to keep them lit. Just then, Al came down. He knew; I could tell. He knew we were fucking up. Al knew everything. Behind Al stood Woofman, inspecting the situation, as if he knew a fucking thing. The whole catastrophe began to overwhelm me. I began to cuss my brains out, hoping that this would confuse Al and show him that I was strong enough to work through any problem. He smiled at this.

"You guys got it covered down here?" Al asked. I could tell he knew we were behind.

"Yeah," Wally answered.

"Looks like a mess down here," Woofman chimed in. I instantly spun my head around and gave Woofman a look of death. He wore a cocky grin.

"You guys know how much you're cooking?" asked Al.

"Yeah. We got all the numbers written down right here." Wally showed Al the distribution chart. Wally was much calmer than I was.

"You just gotta make sure and keep up. Just keep pumpin' out those dogs."

"We got all these ready to go." Wally showed Al the racks ready to go into the grill.

"Just keep pumpin', huh. Pump it. Pump it, baby." Something had gotten into Al. He smiled. He must have been in some good mood because he showed signs of positive enthusiasm.

"We're pumpin'," Wally echoed.

"Oh, yeah. Pumpin'." Al carried on with his "pumpin'" all the way back up the stairs to the concourse. Al had come down to the grill to show concern. Woofman egged his concern on with stupid remarks, and Al walked away a happy man. It was strange, but he must have had some faith in us. Just days earlier, Al told someone, "I'm gonna bash your fuckin' head in." Al's mood was usually poor. Very rarely did something make him happy. The arrival of Al usually meant that you were fucked. He didn't put up with excuses—they were irrelevant. But today he just wanted us to pump. Had he followed us to the whorehouse? I couldn't figure Al out, but I felt he had some confidence in us. However, I was sure that I was getting fucked by Hitler.

I turned my concentration back to Hitler. Mel came down to see what was going on. He approached, bellowing a preacher's words.

"Hallelujah. What a beautiful day. Thanks be to God." He rolled his fat belly around the grill area promoting the good news of the Lord. "Wally, isn't this a beautiful morning!"

"We're fucked," Wally repeated.

Mel turned serious and said, "The Lord's gonna strike you down for using that language."

"Shut up blacky," Wally blurted.

Mel began to laugh a laugh of the gods. "Hey, whitey, you just keep cookin' those dogs, cuz the Lord's on the black man's side today!" He continued his laughing. Wally broke into laugh also. I could only concentrate on Hitler. "You hear that? You hear that, Hakos? Jesus was a black man!"

"Fuck!" I shouted.

"Hitler not workin', Hakos?" Mel asked.

"Nope."

"That's cuz you white boys down here cuss. That's the devil's work." Mel began to leave in order to get to his new charcoal grill on the other side of the stadium. Since Wally had joined me at Hitler, Al promoted Mel to a special

Sweaty Mascots start Grease Fires

good-old fashioned charcoal grill, where customers walked up and ordered something fresh. "Hakos, you hear what I say?" Mel continued his laughing, "Hitler don't work cuz you whities are sinners." I cracked a smirk just long enough to remember the great joy Mel Belle could bring to a person.

Finally, I got Hitler working to the point that we could cook some food for the concession stands. Kids from around the state enveloped the stadium. They rushed in all directions. We sent cooler after cooler up to the stands. I always wondered what the stand manager thought when he or she opened the lid of the coolers to reveal a massive collection of rubbery hotdogs. Then, disgruntled concession's workers slung the thousands of poorly cooked hotdogs into buns and stuffed them in plastic wrap so the dogs could be crammed into a warmer that dried the moisture straight out of the dogs.

The coolers were so heavy that I didn't think that the runners could carry the dogs all the way to the picnics on the other side of the stadium. Wally suggested getting the truck and piling the coolers into the bed of the truck. The truck was having trouble that week; it was stalling uncontrollably. Wally managed to get the truck to the grill area, with the help of a vendor. Then we stacked the weighty coolers into the bed. Wally jumped in with a couple of runners, but the truck wouldn't start. Fuck... another problem. We lifted the hood, and one of the vendors came over to help us. I dealt with the truck all week and knew that the battery was not connected properly. In past experiences, it proved an easy procedure, but this time we couldn't get it to sit without the connection loosening.

"Hakos, what's up?" the vendor asked me.

"It's this wire on the battery. Can you ni..." I was about to say "nigger rig," but since the vendor was black, I thought this a bad idea.

"What? Nigga' rig it?" the vendor asked.

The fact that he said it confused me. "You can say that?" I asked.

"What? Nigga' rig?"

"Yeah."

"Fuck, I just did."

"Ok. Fuck it. Nigga' rig it."

"Oh, yeah," the vendor said, "get me some pliers, and I can fix this up real good."

The vendor fixed the truck in seconds, and Wally sped off around the stadium.

The day started in such a mess that Wally and I failed to keep track of what we cooked, how much we cooked, or where we sent it. Since we lost track, we ended up cooking as much as we could, never checking to see if we needed any. I was in no condition to think, and neither was Wally. By the sixth inning, we knew we were safe. All the concession stands were stocked, the picnics were over, and the kids had used up all their free Fuzzy Bucks. Wally and I collapsed onto a couple of grease-covered coolers, ourselves also grease-covered. We looked and felt like hell. Mel Belle was right. We were in hell. We joked about the morning, and we told the story over and over again to different people, people we could trust of course. As we joked, I realized that Wally spent the entire time laughing, and I spent the whole time frustrated and worried, and by the time we cooked the last hotdog, we came to the same end—we completed our job.

"You just gotta say 'fuck it,' Hakos," Wally enlightened me.

"Yeah, I guess you're right."

I got home around 6 p.m. that evening. Ricki, who ran the ticket office at the stadium, asked if I wanted to meet some of the other Guitars workers out for a beer. I quickly declined the offer. I took a cold shower and watched with burning eyes as the grease slowly drained away like hot fudge being mixed with ice cream. By 6:30 p.m., I was slipping into bed, and, by 6:31, I was asleep.

18 ALTERNATIVE METHODS

I sat interested, watching the news on a television in Al's office. Carson had called me in to the office as I quickly passed on my way to find Butch about some lighter fluid. The electronic images illustrated a horrendous weather front tearing ass in our direction.

"Well," Carson laughed, "what do you think?" He was joking in the manner he always joked, a sort of sarcastic joke he made obvious through his instant laughing.

I smiled. "That's a whole lotta rain."

"Oh, yeah!" A voice called out behind me. Al entered and plopped in his desk chair. He looked at the television. "Wow! Huh!" He looked at us with a big ass grin. "Wow! Damn! Huh! Goddamn!"

We laughed.

"Hey, Hakos, the toilet wouldn't flush. Go check it out," Al said. He wore a straight face. I left to investigate the toilet.

I entered the small office bathroom. A massive stench of rotten shit took me off guard. I looked in the toilet to find a long snake of a turd. I flushed the turd away—it took several tries. I marched back to Al's office.

When I turned the corner into Al's office, He and Carson laughed hysterically.

"You fix it?" Al asked, wearing a smart-ass grin.

"Yeah." Only later did I come to the conclusion that the whole thing was a joke. Al sent me in there to witness his big-ass turd. I shook my head at myself. I hated the fact that the intimidation I felt from Al kept me from thinking coherently. I needed to relax and learn the game—confidence.

I stood in Al's doorway, waiting for the group sales meeting to start. He wanted all the group sales guys there. I recently hitched up with one of the group sales guys to get a taste of it all. I found the experience rather nerve-racking, seeing how I hardly knew the content included in the Guitars group packages. The whole crew finally arrived.

"I want to make sure we have some plan of attack when we're going into these small fuckin' towns. Shit, there's enough of them. Right. These small fuckin' towns. Huh?" Al blurted.

Dwight, the group salesman who called me out on so many occasions, spoke, "Well, you've gotta go into the chamber of commerce first. Get to know them. Ask them questions; find out what community activities are going on. The chamber people will help you out a lot." His face gleamed a proud ray.

"What do you other guys do?" Al asked. "What? You just stop first thing in the local Dunkin' Fuckin' Donuts and hang there for a couple of hours? Huh?"

Everyone laughed a cautious laugh.

"In some of these small towns, you can probably learn a lot from the people in the Dunkin' Fuckin' Donuts. Fuck, the guy who owns it is probably the same guy who's the fuckin' mayor of the town, huh. Shit. Fuck. Huh? Get inquisitive. Ask questions. Fuck."

This charade continued for a while. I understood little. After some time, I zoned out and took in Al's room. The whole thing looked a mess. Proposals here; souvenirs from clients there; something to do with business deals and sales were scattered everywhere. Al really knew no life outside his office. He always sat in this little box with his little

Sweaty Mascots start Grease Fires

windbreaker and his little penetrating eyes. He constantly emitted a heinous body odor, and he enjoyed that. When he dressed up in a tie, he looked awful.

Carson stood close to Al, laughing at his jokes and making witty remarks enjoyed only by Al. Dwight sat with his big belly and bald head, leading the group sales in arrogance. The whole meeting felt creepy. The methods of sales, the interest in selling and the need to invent newer and better ways of selling sank hard in my gut and caused a wicked nausea. I had no interest in the whole "sales" thing.

I struggled with my thoughts... Sell baseball? Why? Who wants to bring their company picnic here? What a rip-off. How do you sell a rip-off? Manipulation.

I just waited for the meeting to end, and that was all that concerned me. I had work to do. I needed to find Butch.

I caught up with Butch a little while later, after giving Mel Belle a jump-start at Hitler. One of my newest duties was setting up the Backyard Grill, as well as Hitler. Eventually, once I organized it, Mel Belle managed the cooking at the Backyard Grill, and I was supposed to oversee both grills. But for now, I ran both directly. Unfortunately, the last home stand zapped us dry of lighter fluid. Somehow, I forgot this in between home stands. This is why I searched for Butch. Finally, we crossed paths. He was just finishing touring a possible client around, a guy with serious spending bucks. This client wanted to pump some cash into the Guitars for some on-field promotional gimmick—great recognition in the minors. Homerun fence signage might be the only thing better. Butch and his client discussed the basics.

"Perhaps, we could do one of those silly things with the fat sumo costumes," suggested the client.

"Totally," Butch responded, "there's millions of possibilities. Let me get with Al and see what we can come up with."

"Right. And I'll talk it over with some of my people. We want something that really catches the fans' attention and screams our name."

Finally, Butch showed him out and caught up with me. Game-time neared, and the backyard grill needed to get up and running.

"We're out of lighter fluid," I said.

"None?"

"None."

"I thought there was some stored up in stand six."

"Nah, I checked. I could run to the store. They probably have some at the gas station." My words sailed right past Butch. He was thinking.

"We don't have time for this. Got it! Run down to the garage," he pointed toward the grounds crew shed, "grab some gasoline and get back here."

I ran and reached the garage. It smelled of mowed grass. I grabbed a full tank of gasoline and jiggled my may back up to the Backyard Grill, consistently losing my balance due to the sloshing of the gas. Butch ran from the concession stand across the way to meet me. He quickly grabbed the tank of fuel and poured it on the charcoal. He took the lighter and touched it to the gasoline-bathed charcoal.

"BOOM!" roared the coals. Each and every piece of coal ignited simultaneously, sending one huge belch of flame into the sky. Butch and I shielded our faces and twisted our backs in a stretch for safety. The flame quickly fell, and the scent of gasoline loomed in the air.

Butch turned to me and laughed a loud laugh with his mouth wide-opened, "That got it!"

I smiled and agreed. But how good can hotdogs smoked in gasoline flavored charcoal be?

As game time neared, I looked to the skies. The smell of gasoline hung in the air. In the sky, dark colors hung heavy with moisture like a hillbilly's beer gut.

Is it gonna rain? I dreamed and kept dreaming, Please rain. Let us go home early. If it does rain, rain now, so we don't have shit loads of cooked hot dogs to sell to no one.

The game began and so did the rain. Umbrellas sprung up all through the stands. The rain pecked at our hotdogs as we took them from the mouth of Hitler. Sizzles of steam poofed in the air with each direct hit. It looked as though the umpire would call for the tarp at any moment. Many of my fellow employees stood at the opposite end of the field, close by the tarp, waiting for the call from the umpire. I held a rack of cooked dogs.

"Let's do it!" The call came over the radio. Everyone rushed to the tarp, which was coiled up around a massive metal tube resembling a hair-roller. I dropped my rack, gave the reigns of Hitler to one of my more capable runners.

I splashed across the wet field and joined the others. We put our fat, baseball-bodied brawn behind the coiled tarp and pushed. Heave! We rolled that bastard out into the outfield, spreading the mammoth sheet across the field. When the tarp was stretched across the outfield, we ran back to the tarp, which now lay folded on only part of the infield. We each grabbed a piece of the tarp so that we could evenly pull it across the field. The wind whipped around us and the rain blew sideways. I squinted through my droplet stained glasses.

The crowd watched in amusement. We grabbed our portion and pulled toward the first base line. The wind blew harder, and we needed to lean into each step. Suddenly, a harsh spit of wind got underneath my section. Several of us lost our grip. The tarp flew 20 to 30 feet up into the air, wiggling in a dance before dropping back down. We gained our hold and tamed the wild tarp. The fans cheered. Once we reached our first base line, we pulled this way and that in order to correctly position the tarp. Then, we raced back across the tarp and pulled the remaining third of it toward left field, adequately covering the infield dirt. I ran across at full speed, knowing that I needed to quickly get back to the grill. I hit a slick spot and slid on my ass into a muddy puddle. The fans roared with laughter. We managed the other side and then staked down the unruly tarp with gigantic nails. I ran back to the grill and attempted to get an idea of where my production was. Rain delays did not mean that food production stopped. If anything, food demand increased because all of the fans took shelter on the concourse. What else to do but eat?

During the delay, the Rodriguez brothers strolled on down to the grill and asked for some pollo. I made them up a plate, and they devoured it in no time, joking all the while, though I hadn't a clue what they said. "Hakos! Chingar la perro!"

After going through my numbers a third time in an attempt to figure where the goods had been sent and how long the food had been in the grill, the skies cleared and the umpire called for the tarp to be removed. I ran back out to the field. We reversed the process, lined up the large hair roller and removed the heavy tarp. When rolling the tarp back onto the large, metal hair roller, we first rolled it unevenly, causing several folds of the tarp to bunch up on one side and hang over the roller. We backed up our rolling and started a second time. This time we got it. Great cheers erupted from the crowd. The game continued...

19 SMASH UP DERBY

With the arrival of coworkers my age came an increase in weekend adventures. Previously, I was quite alone during the weekends and usually did things like watch movies or sleep. Ricki and I usually frequented a restaurant nearby our cockroach-infested apartment. For the most part, we did little else. Usually, we coolly threw back ice-cream sandwiches and watched awful programs like Buffy the Vampire Slayer. Soon enough though, a team of three emerged—Todd, Wally, and me. We found great joy in visiting the Southtown bar scene, and what a scene it was. We became regulars at just about every joint. After games, we usually joined some of the other employees at the taco joint, Taco Company, where we bought far more buckets-o-beer than we ever did tacos. It's an insane thought, but we actually went out after games, after grilling thousands of pieces of meat and cleaning scummy stands. I don't know where we got the energy.

After a long home stand, we finally had a weekend night off. Todd, Wally, and I decided to jazz it up and tour the late night venues of Southtown. We ended up at some dance joint, not our usual cup of tea. Todd and Wally matched up with a couple of hotties on the dance floor, boogying to the usual 70's dance hits. I found myself watching a midget hip-hoppin' on the bar, literally, on the bar. Dressed in an M&M costume, this little man danced his bootie off, while half-naked women cheered him on with raised glasses. The vision mesmerized me. Eventually, I broke myself from the dreams of being a midget long enough to catch a glimpse of Todd and Wally getting down with a couple of babes. I decided to join them, but I wasn't much into playing by the rules on this night. I began dancing in between the couples. Then, I started going through their legs so I could look up the girls' dresses. Perhaps this was juvenile. I thought it was fun. The girls, on the other hand, became annoyed and left. I apologized to the guys. They both claimed they didn't give a shit, and we decided to go. As we left, something hit Todd. He went loony. Perhaps it was my antics in the bar, I don't know. But he lost his mind. Both he and Wally were pretty trashed. I stopped drinking after my infatuation with the midget. I thought it would be best if I drove the drunkards home. Todd began repeating, "Fuck this, man." He had lost his mind. He jumped in his car and peeled off. I told Wally to get in my car.

"He's in no condition to be driving," I said, and Wally and I drove off. "What got into him?"

"I don't know. He's pissed or something."

We lost Todd around a curb as he sped off at a ridiculous speed. I figured he was going home so I took that route. I turned to talk to Wally; he was passed out. I rolled my eyes at the stupidity of the moment and kept driving. I launched onto the interstate ramp and sped onto the empty road. Then I noticed a car at the side of the road. Was it Todd? I couldn't tell in the dark. I continued driving. When we reached Todd and Wally's apartment, I woke up Wally, and I walked in the apartment with him. Wally noticed that there was a message on the machine:

"Wally," the message was distorted by the passing of cars from highway traffic, "I'm fucked. I fuckin' fucked up my car dude." It was Todd, slurring out a jumbled message. He gave us his location, and I figured that it was his car that I saw on the side of the road. I told Wally that

I would go get him, and I sped off, back onto the interstate.

There! I spotted Todd's car. Now, all I had to do was get off the interstate and get back on going the opposite direction. I managed this and pulled up behind Todd's car. My headlights illuminated the inside of Todd's car, but I saw no head. I struggled to see if he was in the car. Just then, I spotted a police cruiser far behind me with its lights flashing. Afraid that I would get caught—I was hardly sober—I threw my car into drive and drove away. The cop sped past me. I got off at the next exit and turned around again, repeating the same routine. This time, I pulled behind Todd's car, got out, and peered into the car. No Todd. I worried, Where the fuck is the bastard? I was getting nervous. I opened his car door, and there, with his seat completely reclined, lay a slumbering Todd.

"Todd!" No reaction. "Todd!"

He raised his head, "Hakos, what's going on." He was completely out of it.

"C'mon." I helped him up and guided him to my car. Looking at his car, there appeared to be no damage. He slumped in his seat, and I hurriedly drove away from Todd's car. I looked over at Todd who was turning his head in either direction, attempting to make sense of the current situation.

"Fuck. I fucked my car up didn't I?" he finally said.

"I don't know. It looked fine to me."

"Did it?"

"Yeah."

"Fuck. No man. It's not fine." Images of what had happened began to hit him. "Fuck! Fuck! Hakos, you know what I did?"

"Huh?"

"I was drivin' and then all of a sudden I was ridin' the guard rail. All these sparks were flyin' all over. I must have fallen asleep. Then some dude told me my tires were flat. That's when I pulled over. Fuck!" I could tell Todd was very upset.

I drove him home, and the next morning we drove back to the spot where we left his car. It was gone. We ended up having to go to the pound of forgotten cars. What seemed like millions of cars littered the lot. Some cars looked completely destroyed, undrivable. Other cars looked fine. The three of us walked up and down the aisles of cars with scraps of past cars crumbling below our feet. We found Todd's car and changed the tire. I couldn't tell in the dark of the night, but the morning sun showed a horrendous mark along the side of Todd's car.

"Hakos, do you know what could've happened?" Todd kept saying.

"No shit." I was disappointed that Todd had done something so stupid. But we had all done something stupid. We just happened to get away with it.

20 INTERN MADNESS

Al decided to place me in charge of our new shipment of interns. I practically was an intern. In fact, my job was worse than any intern... working at the grill, picking up trash, visiting schools, delivering schedules, cleaning the sky boxes—these were all shit jobs that I could claim having done. I still worked alongside the Rodriguez brothers on several occasions.

The Guitars hired about seven interns for this season, and most all possessed a certain arrogant air about them. They seemed to think they deserved something. "I don't have to do this." "This job is shit! I'm not gonna do this." They thought they should be treated as equals to the rest of the staff. Maybe they should have been. But I remember doing the shittiest of all jobs during my previous year. I was still doing them. I never once bitched about having to do it—I just did it. The only thing I bitched about at this point in my career was the fact that the interns were so full of themselves and self-glorifying. Perhaps the interns did deserve better. Perhaps I was just a pushover, allowing myself to be abused. But I believed in taking on my job and doing my best no matter what the job was. I believed bitching showed signs of weakness. This philosophy is probably all wrong. As I have grown older, I have seen the people who believe they deserve better achieve what it is they think they are entitled to. On the other hand, the quiet, obedient people usually remain in that position, and they never achieve the highest ranks. Whether you believe or not, and I'm not even sure I know what I believe today, the attitude of the interns enraged me. I found them to be weak and loud.

Ok, not all the interns acted in this miserable manner. Some followed my lead and worked their shirts to scraps. I appreciated the few who took this attitude, and we hung out quite a bit. We built our crew around the idea that we would make the most of the back-breaking job. Where we could, we made fun out of the whole ridiculous situation.

Two of my favorites, Ken and Brad, really helped me. I pawned most of my shit jobs on them, and they did them without much whining. Shit jobs included playing Fuzzy and working at the grill. Sure, I was still involved in these jobs, but these two guys took a lot of the pressure off me in regards to Fuzzy. They took turns swapping the dreadful job that was Fuzzy. This was not why I liked them though. I liked them because they were somewhat off the wall, like me. And, even though I was made fun of initially for hanging out with the interns, I maintained a close tie to them both.

One of our jobs was cleaning skyboxes. Many of the skybox patrons were slop-messy bastards, leaving us cleaners plenty to freshen. The greatest part of this job was that no one really knew how long the process should take, not even Al. This allowed us to take as much time as we wanted. Plus, most of the boxes were stocked with munchies and various beverages. We often took breaks, lounging in the better boxes, eating their food and drinking their sodas. Ken, Brad, and I even created a little snack band. The sounds and techniques of the snack band were way ahead of their time. Squeezing bags of chips became a great percussion instrument. Spoons and forks added to the drumming. Sporadic voice inflections became the melody. Whatever was in the press box, or whatever ludicrous thing we could think of was included in our band. I'm pretty sure we could have toured with our sound. It was original and crunchy.

The skybox-cleaning boys also created the Imitation Cleaning Method. It was difficult to see the people cleaning the skyboxes from the field, but they could be seen nonetheless. So, when taking breaks, the cleaning crew pretended to work. The person with the vacuum rolled the machine back and forth without it even being on. The people with the rags repeatedly rubbed the same ashtray. All the while, the cleaning crew was either talking or singing. Rather than bitch about their work, the interns I appreciated made the most of their work. In fact, they revolutionized their jobs, adding flare that human resource directors should integrate into the workplace.

During many of the off days, Al placed me in charge of organizing a plan for distributing schedules. I called it Operation Saturation. I usually sent Brad and Ken out together. Through my scientifically organized saturation agenda, the interns dispersed enough schedules around Southtown to last the city into the next century. I am sure today, people in Southtown still find 1998 Guitars schedules inhabiting their place of work when cleaning desk drawers and fishing around the space between the water cooler and the wall. Of course, much of the interns' time was spent not saturating the city. Some of the time was spent in movie theaters or playing video games in some monstrosity of an audio/video store.

I remember one time, while on a Saturation mission, I stumbled across a church in a nearby town. I decided to see if they would be interested in a picnic. I parked my car and took a walk. It felt good to get on my feet after so much driving. I checked the side door of the church, and it opened. I walked in and and looked around. I walked to the office, but nobody was there. I opened the doors that led to the chapel, and I saw a variety of instruments lining the front. There was the traditional piano and organ, but there were also a vibraphone, guitar, drums, harp, bass, and many others. Since no one was home, I figured they wouldn't mind if I played around a little. I immediately jumped on the vibraphone and jammed out something comparable to the chord structure invented by a two-year-old. I played some drums and strummed the harp. After a couple minutes of inventing my own one-man band, I took out from my bag some information on Guitars picnics. I thought I could enlighten them with the joy of minor league baseball. Perhaps this could be part of the next sermon. I neatly gathered some information and laid it delicately on the altar. There, a sign from above. How could they resist a Guitars picnic now? I genuflected and quietly left.

21 CHANGES

During my second season, Butch became increasingly disenchanted with the way the Guitars treated him. He felt Al kept good sales leads from him. Butch decided he wanted to concentrate on sales and promotions, but he couldn't do his best without being given adequate leads. Midway through the season, Al placed Wally in charge of concessions (which made things very interesting due to Wally's love for increased challenges). Al removed Butch from the concessions, and Butch, though he claimed he didn't want the position anymore, seemed more and more depressed. He frequently visited my apartment drunk, spilling out his grievances.

"Al didn't do shit in the army," Butch ranted, "He didn't see any action." His face scowled. "One time, we were woken in the dead of night. We didn't know what the fuck was going on. We were told we got a mission. I was scared as shit. We jumped in these helicopters and were raced off somewhere." Butch's army story included gunfire and near misses, and I had heard it all before.

I felt bad for Butch. Though we didn't really hang out any longer, I still held Butch in high esteem. Butch began looking for another job, and he soon left the Guitars.

I learned a lot from Butch. I learned about confidence, trust, and hard work. I also learned his temper. I took after

Butch, yelling at people and throwing things. I never did these things in the past, but I saw how intimidating Butch was to others, and I wanted to emulate that. I thought it was the best way to get people to listen to me. Heck, it worked for Al. Before, I thought things out and paused before reacting to a frustrating situation. Now, I reacted with instant anger.

The end of the second season was a confusing one. The ownership was in disarray, revenues were low, and the blame was being placed on Al. The director of group sales told us that Al would soon be gone—fired. Al continued his work though and sent us out around Southtown, collecting and distributing information. The director of group sales told us in secret that things were going to change once Al was gone. He told us to go out and pretend that we were working. I didn't mind this at all, but I also didn't know how to feel about it.

I took advantage of the administrative turmoil, making leisurely deliveries of sales information in between going to the movies and taking long lunches.

The owners came down one afternoon and told the staff that Al wanted to move on, and they were sorry to see him go. This was definitely bullshit. We knew differently. (In fact, I came to the conclusion that every time there is some press conference where someone is leaving under his or her own free will, they are not.) Soon, Al was gone and we were left without a general manager. Now, there was no one to guide us. There was no one to instill fear within us. For the longest time, the staff was a bunch of loose cannons, drifting about the office without direction, and drifting about sales calls without drive—I had never spent so much time at the theaters.

With Al went Woofman. I don't think anybody was sorry to see this guy go. He still had jobs performing at Minor League games with his dog, but he was gone from the Southtown Guitars. Well, not really gone. He kept showing up, taking up space in the concessions office. I'd be on the phone trying to make a sale, and he'd barge in

Sweaty Mascots start Grease Fires

blurting, "Hey, ah, what the fuck's goin' on?" Usually, he kept talking to me even when I tried to talk on the phone. I hoped every day that Woofman never showed up ever again. His presence irritated and scared me at the same time.

Finally, I had had enough. I got the nerve to clear off his desk and make it mine. I took all of his useless wires and nails and threw them in a box. From one drawer I pulled a moldy cup; from another a scratched picture of him and a Hooters girl; and why did he need nail polish? I cleared the desk and cleaned it of Woofman's stench. The desk was mine. I never saw The Woof again.

Life at the Guitars was changing quickly. Was it for the better? Some thought so. Some didn't. If you were part of the old crew, hired under Al in the first year, like I was, you felt some disappointment about the changes. We grew to appreciate (though equally fear) the organization style of Al. He got things done, even if it was a bit unorthodox. At the same time, gone were the excruciating work days under Al. Alive was a more by-the-book and crisper style of work. If you were part of the new work crew, many interns included, you probably liked the changes. Whatever the case, the changes made it difficult to know what to do and who to listen to.

The confusion continued during the off-season. I was placed in sales, where I was in charge of church outings and little leagues. It was horrible! Remember my church altar strategy? Not good. I was a horrible speaker, and usually I fumbled through a stumbling of informative phrases. I probably confused people more than informed them.

My stomach knotted up each morning with the thought of the day's sales meetings. Next thing I knew, I found myself slowly driving, looking for the correct address of a manufacturer of somethingorother. I drove and drove. Time passed, and I drove. The meeting was in five minutes. My leg nervously bounced in an attempt to speed my arrival. A wrong turn and another, and the sting of sweat began. I turned the radio off, and I sat up against the steering wheel in the hopes that a more engaged attitude would find the church. Finally, ten minutes late, I sped into the parking lot and quickly appeared at the front desk. I greeted the receptionist with a sweaty smile. I held the signature bag of peanuts in one hand and a folder of information in the other. The receptionist giggled. I must have looked like the most uncomfortable and unqualified sales specimen. My lack of confidence wrapped tightly around my neck, increasing my vocal pitch by an octave. With my elfish voice, I asked to see the person in charge of group outings.

"Oh, that would be Dick Flabfucker," she said (I don't remember his real name).

I waited around for Dick, and finally he swung with his almighty self, flashing his brilliance. I squinted, and he walked by; his strut pulled me in, and I followed Dick to his enormous office. He sat me down at one end of the room, and a couple of minutes later he made his way behind his corporate desk. I could hardly see him. I adjusted my glasses.

"So, you're with the Guitars, eh?"

"Yes."

"How long ya been there?"

"Two seasons."

"Guitars suck."

"Well, I don't know..."

"I remember when they were owned by that other guy in the 80's, and they kicked ass. You were probably just a baby at that time." Flabfucker swiveled himself around in his chair to admire his office. I waited. His pause gave me enough time to consider his comment. He was probably a few years older than me, making us nearly the same age in the 1980s. So, if I was a baby, he was too. But I wasn't a baby; I was entering high school in the 80s. This guy was probably a senior when I was a freshman, and he probably would have been one of those dickheads who pissed on me just to make himself feel better.

He continued, looking down at me over his round belly, "Now, if I go for this group plan, and I bring 200 of my employees, that'll come out to..." his fingers magically brushed across his dumb calculator, "...about $2,500."

"Yeah, I guess that's right."

"You guess? Ha. Hakos you're gonna have to do better than 'guess' to sell me. You know why?"

I bet you'll tell me. I could have said anything at this point. He was too impressed with himself to hear me.

"If you look at this 10-person group plan and look at this picnic plan that you're trying to sell me for, you guess, $2,500, you can find a flaw. Or maybe you can't find a flaw, but I can."

"What's that?"

"If I take 20 of these 10-person group plans, which come with dogs and soda, I'm getting away with $2,000 instead of $2,500."

I was confused as hell. I really had no response. I was not a salesman, and I certainly didn't want to go to the effort of thinking of a response for this arrogant ass. He smiled at me with an air of victory. In all honesty, he blew me away. He lived for this, and when it came time to play the game, he played it a hell of a lot better than I did. This was his love, and I couldn't have cared less. If he wanted to find cheap loopholes, it was fine with me. I wasn't about to compete in some game of corporate arrogance. I really just wanted the day's work to be done so I could go home.

"Can I do that?" he asked.

"I don't see why not. You won't get the coleslaw, which comes with the picnic."

"I don't like coleslaw, Hakos."

"Well maybe some of your employees do."

"Hakos, I'm the director of HR. I review the work of over 200 employees each year. I sit down with each of them, explaining what it is they could do to do better. I know them. I know them better than my wife and newborn baby. If coleslaw was a high priority, I'd know."

Flabfuck kept talking, looking to the ceiling for inspiration. Perhaps he felt the majesty of God, or perhaps he felt like God. Maybe he was God, and if that's true, then sign me out. Whatever the case, we began talking religion.

"So you sell to churches too?" he said examining his nails, "I don't understand religion. Are you religious?"

"I don't know if I'm religious, but I consider myself a Catholic."

"Consider yourself, eh? I don't get it. Why worship Mary? She didn't do anything. You expect me to believe that some virgin had a baby?" To these questions, I had no response. I had been humiliated enough. "I'm not trying to bash your religion, Hakos, but it just doesn't make sense to me." At this point in my life, I had yet to truly evaluate my religion. I admit. I didn't have any answers, and I didn't really care. Was he gonna buy some tickets or not. I had another meeting, and I wanted to get lunch.

He kept talking, and I listened for a while, until I realized he was holding a conversation with himself, and I let him. His voice faded to the background, and I took to examining his enormous desk and little trinkets. Every once in a while I'd catch some of his rant, and I'd nod. When he was finally pleased with himself, I left.

He called me at the office with new numbers and better prices he found by combining ticket plans. By the end, I just held the phone away from my ear, and I gave him whatever he wanted. The best part about it though, is that he canceled his picnic after spending so much of his time trying to figure the best deal.

I did get many groups to sign up for blocks of tickets and picnics. Well, I didn't really have much to do with the commitment. Most of the groups had been coming to Guitars games for years. I was merely providing them with the contract and taking it back to the ticket office. I was nothing more than a messenger. I took a piece of paper there, and I brought it back here. Groups didn't sign on the line because of my charisma or rhetoric. Groups signed because that's what the group picnic had been and there was no interest in changing it. I guess you could say that I was really good at keeping the status quo. All of my attempts to reach out and gain a new client went up in flames.

I entered this guy's church office. It was some Baptist Church that resembled something more like a corporate headquarters for God. And this is what the guy said:

"I admitted you this afternoon because I had a vision. Sit down." I sat, though he would not have noticed since his eyes were looking up into the sky as his hands massaged the air in front of him. "In my vision, God told me that a messenger was going to come today." He turned to me, "Hakos, you're the messenger. Isn't it amazing?" I just sat and examined his overly pressed shirt, designer glasses and well groomed facial hair. He turned back to the ceiling. "Hakos, I need an event to capture the faiths of youngsters. I believe heavily in outreach, and I know that's why you're here. I feel really excited about it." He turned back to me, "Hakos, can we put something big together?"

"Sure. Big." I actually felt excited. I hadn't sold anything big. This was my big chance to make a name for myself in the group sales.

"I'm thinking a concert on the infield, where thousands of adolescents attend. Can you do that?"

"I'd imagine we could work something out." I had no fucking clue.

"Cuz, as you can see, Hakos, I have an enormous church." He disclosed some outrageous number of faithful in the congregation. "It is a beautiful specimen of God. I believe I can fill that stadium if this is done right."

"Great."

"I know some people in the music industry. Now, we couldn't have just anybody play. We'd need some big names to get the kids out there." He mentioned some religious country bands and told me that they were big.

He told me more about the vision, and then he changed directions. "Hakos, do you attend church?"

"Yes, I do as a matter of fact."

"What church?"

"I go to a couple actually. There are a couple of nice Catholic Churches around."

"Catholic? Well, that's okay. But you seem like you're searching for something."

"Really?" The funny thing was that I was searching for something at this time. I had been reading into the gospels more. I was in search of some understanding of the world around me—perhaps a clue as to why I was in baseball.

"Yes. Are you searching?"

I decided to play along. There was something that I had been wondering about. There is a passage in the Gospel of Luke that talks about surviving through perseverance. I tried to describe it the best I could. "I think it goes something like, 'Through patient perseverance you will survive.'" I wanted to know what he thought that meant.

He searched his brain and said, "I'm not familiar with that one. I think you need to search further."

I felt dumb. I played along. I reached out, and I my inquiry was rejected. Another person who didn't listen. He just talked.

"Hakos, let me put some numbers together. I'm thinking 4,000 at the least."

He kept talking, but I was stuck on 4,000. I expressed no emotion, but inside, I was bubbling, and it felt kind of good. 4,000!

"I'll give ya a call later in the week. We can meet again, and finalize some details." His eyes again read the ceiling's creases. I followed, but saw nothing.

We met several times, and with each meeting, I became ever more disenchanted. One meeting at Southe restaurant, he got pissed with the waitress for being slow. This didn't seem like something Jesus would have done, and I had to question his intentions. After that, the whole thousands of dollars idea flopped. No concert ever occurred and no adolescents ever attended any outing. His

Sweaty Mascots start Grease Fires

vision from God never materialized. I guess I was a fallen angel.

Each night I collapsed in wonder. I was not a salesman. I lacked the drive and killer instinct. A few months before the next season, I had it in my mind to quit. The whole game was getting old.

Concurring events failed to motivate me. On one occasion, I decided to drive north to Clarksville, where the parents of one of my friends from college lived. My friend's father ran a business up there, and I thought this meeting might shed some light. Perhaps he might condone my job. Perhaps he might give me another job or some satisfying advice. I took it upon myself to make this one of my sales calls. I presented myself at the front desk, and my friend's father promptly accepted me. He showed me into his office, and I seated myself opposite his magnificent desk. The last time I saw this guy I was wearing only a bathrobe. He reminded me of this. He asked how I was, and I gave the usual response. He told me a bit of what he did, and then he asked me about Southtown. He wondered if there were any corporate headquarters there.

"I don't know, really. Like in Akron, you have Goodyear. I don't know about Southtown," I said.

"I don't see how a city can maintain itself without a strong central business like Goodyear."

"I don't know," I told him.

A lot of this "I don't know" business happened, and finally he asked me about the Guitars. I told him my duties of grilling and stocking stands. I tried to decorate them a tad by leaving out some of the more hideous details. He sat on the other side of his desk, in his leather chair, and pondered my words. He looked at me with a dad's look, where the hand massages the face, rolling up the fat in the cheeks.

"I think you can do more than this, Hakos," my friend's dad said. He added, "You didn't go to college for this job. You probably didn't even have to go to college for this job."

Had he been talking to my dad? Whatever the case, it didn't matter. I understood his point and agreed with him. I sat stiff, nodding my head. "Yeah," I incessantly replied.

No job offer or praise came from the meeting, just a pat on the back and a self-guided walk back down the hall to the lobby. I bid the man goodbye and went on my way. I drove away completely empty. Back to Southtown.

I reached the office early, as usual. Reading over the paper, I saw that Clarkesville had been obliterated by a tornado. I thought to call my friend's dad, but it was too early in the morning. Instead, I sat back in the squeaky office chair and took a moment to ponder. Should I quit? Many of my friends had already left the Guitars. Butch was gone, and Wally was offered a general manager job out west. Wally said something to me as he was leaving, "Hakos, you're gonna get stuck here. Are you gonna work here forever? I'm gonna come back here years from now, and you're still gonna be here. You'll be some old man working at the grill." Wally imitated me at 80, and we had a laugh. But he was right. Was I going to put up with this shit forever? I hated the sales part. Concessions was hell. Even without the pressure from Al, I was afraid of everything. I had become accustomed to hating and fearing my job, but I began to think that this was just the way work was and that I better quit whining about it and gird up my loins.

22 WEEKEND SANITY

I really looked forward to the weekends. Weekends during the off-season were usually free, and this freedom was enough to keep me going from week to week. With the departure of Wally from Southtown, Todd and I bonded more than ever before. Ricki moved in with another friend of his, and I took Wally's room in Todd's apartment. We both enjoyed live concerts, and we decided to get tickets to a Phish show at Southtown's big outdoor amphitheatre. We first stopped into a local bar by Todd's apartment to have some crawfish and brews. The crawfish seemed a nice beginner to a Phish concert that we knew would focus primarily on getting lit. We finished our liquid-heavy dinner and headed toward the concert. As we exited the bar, we bumped into some people from the Guitars. Todd and I babbled nonsensicals and stumbled to our car. Todd broke out his flask while in the car, and we began taking frequent swigs of whiskey. We were already well on our way to getting trashed and I find that speedy drunkenness provides the greatest excuse for continual drinking. We arrived at the amphitheatre and bought ourselves some beer. We roamed around the grassy hill for a while before selecting the perfect spot to lay our blanket and chairs. The first beer quickly disappeared, and we headed for more. We noticed some people crawling around some bushes so we decided to join them. We lifted up some hefty branches and squatted our way into the bushes. We introduced ourselves to a nice looking young lady who promptly offered us some illegal particulars. I declined, while Todd partook. We began a long discussion about this girl's pursuits in leisure.

"Wrestlin' 'n racin'...that's what I like," she said.

"You mean like pro-wrestling?" Todd sounded disappointed.

"Ah, yeah, man. I like NASCAR even more."

"I don't get the point of NASCAR," I said.

"What's not to get? Fast fuckin' cars racin' around a track," she answered.

"Exactly. Around a track. The cars just fuckin' go around a track," Todd blurted, and I added a circular motion with my hand.

"I just like those fuckin' fast-ass cars." The girl's face showed signs of rage as she imagined herself in the driver's seat of a racecar.

I looked down at my beer and noticed that it was empty. "I gotta get another beer. I'll be back." I left Todd to argue wrestlin' and racin' with the girl. I made my way to a concession stand and stood back, watching the activity of the stand. I examined the workings inside the stand and realized that it resembled a stand at our baseball stadium. Then, I thought, those employees are just like my concessions employees. They could probably give a shit. I can walk in there untouched. I knew the concession stand workers wouldn't think twice if some unknown person walked inside. I decided to give it a shot. I walked into the stand and looked around. Nobody even looked at me. I decided to go further, testing the water. I took a pretzel from the pretzel display and took a bite. The pretzel was cold in the middle. I got the attention of a girl working in the stand and said, "Hey, those pretzels are still frozen. You need to run those through the warmer again."

Sweaty Mascots start Grease Fires

"Okay," she replied and began taking the pretzels out of the display and running them through the warmer. With that, I was in. I decided to go the distance.

How about these dogs? Are these dogs done? I pulled a hotdog from the warmer and took a bite. Pretty good. I looked at another kid and said, "Nice job."

This was so easy. With a little bit of knowledge on my part and a whole lot of stupidity on the workers' part, I successfully ransacked the concession stand. I grabbed a pretzel that had been placed on the warmer again and took a bite. "Much better." I looked around the stand for the walk-in cooler. I moved to the back of the stand, always looking confident, and found the cooler. I walked in and began looking around. I didn't know what I was going to do in there, but I thought I might be able to take a pack of beer if it was lying about, or even a keg. Just then, a man walked in.

"What are you doing in here?" I could tell he was the stand manager, and he was pissed. I bent over to check the hose connection of the keg.

"Yep. These kegs are all hooked up right," I said.

"Course they are," he barked back.

"And the cooler...good temperature. You're doing a fine job."

"Look. I've been here for eight years, and there has never been anything wrong with my stand."

"Oh, no, I wouldn't doubt it. This is well kept."

"Who are you?"

"Hah. Sorry I didn't introduce myself. I'm with the Pittsburgh Pirates staff. We were down here checking out the Southtown Guitars concessions, and we heard there was an event going on here. So, I called up Ken Worscher," I paused for a moment and continued, "you know Ken don't ya?"

"Sure," the bastard answered, which was total bullshit because I just made the name up on the spur of the moment.

"Yeah, well Ken asked us to come down here and check out some of his concession stands." I took another look around and continued, "All this looks good though. I'm impressed." I started my exit out the cooler. "This is a fine establishment. Thanks for your help. See ya." I left the stand manager baffled in the cooler. What an idiot. I grabbed a hotdog on my way out and walked back to Todd.

When I reached the bushes, Todd and the girl were both gone. I walked to our blanket and Todd was standing there. Phish had started without me realizing it.

"Todd."

"Yeah?"

"You need a beer?"

"Yeah."

Again, I walked off. I entered another concession stand and also told my fake story to a lemonade vendor. I roamed the whole place, selling my story to whomever I could. Right after I got a free flavored pretzel, the sky exploded and rain appeared, immediately falling like buckets.

"Fuck. I gotta get to the car." I began running with my lemonade and pretzel through the grass to the parking lot. The only problem was that I didn't know where the car was from inside the amphitheatre. I only knew where the car was if I drove in through the entrance of the theater parking lot. Therefore, I did the only rational thing. I ran outside one of the exits of the amphitheater and began running down the street toward the road we entered from. It was so wet that I slipped onto the road and lost all of my souvenirs. I slid across the pavement into a gutter. I began laughing hysterically and continued my run. I found the entrance we used, and I followed that road to our parking area. I located the car, and found Todd waiting there.

"Where the hell have you been, man?" he yelled through the pouring rain.

"I didn't know where the car was." I began unlocking the car, fiddling with the key in the rain. A couple of snickers later and the door opened. We jumped inside. I turned to Todd, "The only way I knew was to leave the place and come in the entrance we used." He laughed for a while, and Todd asked if he could use some of the notebook paper I had sitting in my car to roll a joint. I thought it was fine, and Todd began a losing battle of rolling and smoking a joint made of notebook paper. I took another swig of his whiskey on the way home, and he stuck his paper-joint in his hat (Unfortunately, the paper used by Todd included notes on it that were to be used for this story. Those notes burnt away tragically with the joint).

We felt a great, drunken hunger. We stopped at a Steak 'n Shake. Todd got a fuck load of breakfast items, and I got a milk shake. We stumbled back to the car after our meal and continued home. It was 4 a.m. and I was exhausted. I collapsed in my bed and fell soundly asleep. I awoke the next morning trying to put the previous night together. After I recalled most of the night's stupid antics, I realized that I never heard a note of Phish.

Although Todd and I missed most all of Phish, Southtown's live music scene was the place for us. Music constantly excited the streets of Southtown. On one occasion, my cousin, who was visiting from Akron, and I decided to hang out at a small downtown bar, Bob's. We ordered a couple of drinks, talked about our lives, and enjoyed a group of old-fogies scraping together a few old tunes. A night out was never complete without the unforeseen conversation with some straggler at the bar.

"This place is great, ain't it?" spoke the straggler, who wore a loyal cowboy uniform, hat and all.

"Yeah."

"What do you guys do?" We talked briefly about our lives and asked the cowboy to disclose some of his background.

"Ahh, well, I'm in town for the rodeo."

"Really?"

"Yep. I'm in the rodeo."

"You mean you actually ride and lasso cattle?" asked my cousin.

"Shit yeah. I rip down those mothers." He slapped his leg and burst into a good old cowboy shout.

The band finished a song, and we clapped and hollered.

"Most of these places now-a-days are bullshit." He looked around the bar as he said this as if to suggest that all places with the same kind of atmosphere were bullshit. I also noticed that "bullshit" streamed from his mouth with such potency that I wanted to perhaps put it in my drink to spice it up. "Yeah, fuck. It's all bullshit."

Soon enough, we left the cowboy to find another bar. He told us to come to his rodeo, and we said we would try.

"That's bullshit," he joked with a holler.

We left the bar, but on our way out, one of the guys from the band poked his head out of the door and called on us to wait.

"Hey, you that drummer from Bruce Springsteen's band?" he asked my cousin.

"You mean Max Weinburg?" my cousin asked.

"Yeah."

"No," then my cousin pointed to me, "but he plays the drums."

The band member motioned for me to come back, "You wanna play a few songs with us?"

I looked at my cousin who motioned for me to play. So, I marched back into the bar with my cousin following.

I jumped on the miniature stage and greeted the band members. The drummer offered me his place, and I hopped behind the drum kit. Now, I am not too shabby of a drummer, I mean, I think I can hold my own with whatever the moment demands. However, as I took my place behind the drums, I noticed that everything was backward. The high-hat was on the right, and everything looked as though it was in a mirror—flipped image. I was fucked. How could I play a constant and sustained beat with the wrong hands?

"It's a left-handed kit, my friend," said the guitarist, "can you do it?"

I paused a moment, looked at the drums again in order to think it through, and said with shrugged shoulders, "Sure."

"One, two, three, four..." The band strummed into a slow country favorite, and I quickly followed with a simple backbeat. Tense at first, I quickly relaxed into my backward playing. We jammed out a couple of tunes. It was great. During the third song, the band stopped all of a sudden, and I followed, pausing with my drumsticks just above the snare. I glanced up to see what was the matter.

"Keep going," the bassist said with a smile on his face. I took this to mean that I was supposed to pay a solo. I crashed into my drums with all my speed and might. Thrashing my arms around the toms and into the cymbals, I lost myself in a sloppy yet convincing drum solo. During a drum solo, the brain shuts down, and pure instinct guides the drummer for those few seconds as he wails and bashes away, like a melodic herd of horses galloping across the open plains.

When my minutes of fame were up, the band asked the audience to recognize my effort, and the guitarist added, "Not too shabby on a left-handed drum kit."

I thanked the band and jumped off the stage, joining my cousin at the front door. It was fabulous. As I relayed the experience to my cousin, jumbled words bounced from my mouth with excess speed. The feeling was pure joy. I took a deep breath to capture the moment and exhaled it back out into the night. It was a complete rush, a rush of enthusiasm I had not felt for a long time. So this is what joy can be found in a job you love.

PART IV

23 SEASONED FRUSTRATION

Midway through the season, things usually got a little easier. Familiarity set in. The interns knew the routine for unloading deliveries, and the staff evolved into a minor league baseball machine. The hard part was establishing employee cooperation. It took tremendous patience to wait for enough interns to show up to help. The Guitars organization was in such disarray that no department worked together. The concessions department worked separately from the sales department, who worked separately from the promotions departments, and so on. We only communicated to further our own department's goals, and hence, we usually fought for help from the interns—they were like our rag dolls.

I knew a big delivery was coming. I needed a good number of interns. When will it get here? It's already 11 o'clock. Where are those interns? I took refuge from the Southtown heat inside the freezer. I sat on a stack of sausages and reached down into a case of frozen cookies, pulling out a chocolate chip cookie and drowning myself in its goodness. I tried the white chocolate chip cookie next. Soon I received a call on the radio that the delivery arrived. I immediately called on some interns for help. When the interns finally arrived, I took charge, unloading a heavy shipment from our largest food distributor. With me in the delivery truck tossing cases out to the boys below, we cleaned out the frozen foods and packed them onto our pick-up truck. Then we drove down to our freezer by Hitler. I lined up the interns in a long assembly line with me at the end, in the freezer. One by one, the cases of melting frozen foods bounced their way from person to person until I placed the contorted shape of cardboard onto similarly shaped cases.

It took great focus to rotate and balance the products in the freezer. However, the half-melted, abstract shapes of the cases became difficult to stack. Stacks of pretzel cases twelve high leaned to the left with cartoonish impossibilities.

The interns continued to transport cases inside the freezer. The packages of product seemed to melt through our hands in the Southtown sun. The cases that sat in the truck sunk into their own melted ice and condensation. The dirt remaining in the truck from the Rodriguez Brothers' earlier mission of trimming the hedges and mowing the stadium grounds still sat in the bed of the truck and slowly crept onto the cases, kind of like the Blob.

We finished unloading the heavy shipment from the distributor. The interns took the truck back up to the parking lot, ready to accept its next job.

I closed the door to the freezer and remained inside. The temperature quickly dropped, and I plopped myself down on some slushy cases of bratwursts. My allergies acted up in the Southtown heat, and the freezer provided a haven from the annoying sneezing and itchy eyes. I sat and took a deep breath of iced-air. My warm body cooled with frozen sweat. I reached down into a case of cookies again. The cookies arrived in a hockey puck form, frozen and hard. I took a slow bite of the precious cookie. It remained gooey despite the frozen conditions. Mmmmm. A mix of sugar and chocolate cascaded over my tongue, a relaxing moment within a hectic day. Outside the freezer, Hitler heated up, preparing for the onslaught of fans.

Though I still dreaded games and my job, my social life took a more positive turn. Moving in with Todd was the perfect decision. Todd and I bonded during the previous season, and we formed a strong friendship. We began a strict workout schedule, running and lifting weights after work. Together, we slimmed down and toned our muscles. Focusing our attention so strongly on changing our lifestyle helped relinquish the agony of work. In addition, we began eating better. My time spent sweating over beef and wieners took its toll on my taste for certain meats and I slowly began to tiptoe down the vegetarian path. So, for the first time, I found a living situation in Southtown that helped me deal with my job. Todd and I both hated our jobs, and sometimes we sat on our balcony with a bottle of wine and some cigars to talk about life. We told stories and philosophized. Todd told me of better times in his life, and I likewise. It sounds corny, but it was actually my favorite thing to do. It felt liberating to hear about life from someone else's standpoint.

However, even though I loved the living situation, I often locked myself in my room for some peace and quiet. I read, played guitar, or watched movies. I knew Todd thought this was strange. He may have thought I didn't want to be around him, but truthfully, I just wanted time to be me without the craziness of the job. When I allowed it, the job turned me into a hate machine, and I hated that about myself. I rated everything by how much I hated it. Before Southtown, I enjoyed everything. I enjoyed seeing people and talking to them. Now, I had transformed into a pessimistic bastard who hated all things.

My increasing obsession for recreational activities acted as my only outlet from my world of frustration. I reveled in the exercise of drinking, but running became my big getaway. Todd and I found some great places to run in Southtown's parks. Sometimes I went to the park early on the weekends and ran up and around the hilly wilderness. Afterwards, I sat in the grass with my head raised toward the sun. The fresh rays of sun warmed my smiling face, as

I forgot about the bad and concentrated on the beautiful moment at hand.

My job became secondary. I hardly worked as diligently as before, meaning that now I only put in one hundred percent instead of one-fifty. Todd and I and some of the rest of our friends like Ken, Peter, and Brad began finding more things to do outside of work. We took full advantage of every moment away from the stadium. We began going to as many places in downtown Southtown as we could. We frequented the bars that played live Southern music. We even made our way outside of Southtown for some fun.

Todd, Peter, and I drove east on one occasion in pursuit of some hearty camping. It took us longer than we anticipated, and we arrived at our destination after dark. We unpacked our car and got everything ready for walking. Todd flicked on the flashlight, and we began our venture into the black forest. I couldn't see my feet in this darkness. All I could see was the small circle the flashlight created in the distance. It was just one tree after another. Finally, we approached what seemed to be a river, and we stopped for a moment. We each carried a backpack, and Peter and I painstakingly lugged a cooler of beer. This was not working. We turned around and headed back toward the car, where we decided to pitch the tents for the night.

I woke early and built a small fire. The darkened logs still smoked from the fire we made the night before. The smell of a fresh, dewy morning mixed with campfire lifted my spirits. Later, we trekked through the beautiful wilderness. We saw the creek that stopped our advancement and laughed at its miniature width and the fact that it ended our walk. We saw waterfalls and rivers, and we drank from the clearest creek I had ever seen. Finally, we came to a cliff, where we could see for miles. Millions of trees covered the world below. Each of us sat on the edge with our feet dangling high above the tall trees below. We lay back and breathed in the moment. The next thing I knew, I was waking from a nap. We had all fallen asleep on the edge of a cliff, and it was the most beautiful thing. I felt brilliantly refreshed. When we thought about it for a moment, we decided it was ridiculous and scary, but our fear melted, and we could only think of how wonderful it was—purely relaxing. We each took a picture of ourselves in front of the eternal view of the trees that spread as far as I could see. I took one last look, smiled, and walked on through the trees.

Times like these calmed my anxieties and helped me love life, and hate my job even more. The Southtown Guitars was the only bad thing about life at this time, everything else was actually quite marvelous. Unfortunately, I often forgot the joys of life under the stress and depression brought on by my work.

24 IN CHARGE AND HATING IT

My third season saw me placed in charge of the concessions. Well, sort of. The team hired an older more experienced guy to oversee all of the food and beverages, but, quite honestly, I took charge of the concession stands and all food production. My experience surpassed all others at the stadium in this department, and for all intents and purposes, I could calculate the food production without thinking. My superior knew everything there was to know about concessions, like food expos.

A bit on food expos. These food expos are strange events. Johnny and I attended several food expos during the first half of the year with the superior. At the large Southtown convention center, row upon row of food vendors and the like packed themselves tightly together in a battle of persuasion. Up and down the rows we walked, trying everything from special hot dogs to Dip 'n Dots ice-cream. We devoured frozen, fried chicken, fish and fries. We ate my favorite cookies and popped a couple kernels of kettle-corn into our mouths. The superior gave praise to the traditional Cracker Jacks flavor. The superior and Johnny took smoke breaks outside, before coming back for a Dr. Pepper. During one expo, the superior bumped into a friend of his from Hormel.

"Hey buddy." The two shook hands and exchanged pleasantries. The superior turned to us, "These guys do Spam." He pointed to the SPAM shirts sitting on the kiosk.

"Ew," we groaned.

"I love Spam," the superior said.

"I don't know if I've tried it," I confessed.

"Hakos, you're missin' out."

"I'll get you guys some. I'll bring it by the stadium," the representative said. "We have new flavors now." He turned and grabbed a tin of Spam. "Look, Hot 'n Spicy Spam."

"Oh, we gotta try that," the superior said.

Later, I did try Spam when the representative stopped by the stadium with some souvenir t-shirts. Salty shit, that Spam, but it's not that bad. Quite tasty as a sandwich spread.

The superior was a great guy, but his age showed in the relentless baseball life. Since my superior found it difficult to keep pace, the burden fell on me. However, I lacked the strong guidance of Butch I previously relied upon. I was on my own now, or at least I felt on my own. Similar to my belief at the grill, I felt the responsibility to take care of every task myself, now on a much grander scale. My new challenge came in dealing with the employees. We hired a fresh batch of young kids, and I adopted Butch's style of rage to intimidate and keep the kids in line. I wasn't prepared for the backlash.

I overheard one of my coworkers say something sarcastic about me over the radio once. I sought the bastard out and reamed his ass by screeching curses that not even God knows.

"What the fuck did you say?" I questioned my coworker.

"Hey, Hakos, I was only joking," he innocently insisted. He actually was one of my favorite coworkers. However, the stress from the job engulfed my behavior.

"Fuck you if you think I'm not doin' anything. I'm bustin' my fuckin' ass more than you...you fuckin' fat fuck!" My behavior surely was not going to win any awards or friends.

I left the guy stunned, and took off back to my miserable life. Without Al in the scene, I felt I could do anything—nobody was at the top who might punish me for my erratic behavior. In fact, there was nobody at all at the top. I felt at ease in being a cocky asshole.

The fact was that nobody was really willing to fuck with me. I don't know if it was because I really did work my ass off more than anyone else, or if it was because my behavior scared the hell out of them. I was sure, however, that I was once a happy-go-lucky college graduate. Now, two years later, I was fucking insane. I cut the sleeves off my game day shirts. I wore a stained hat from the days of the grill, and my shaving was quite sporadic. Everything about me was sporadic.

During non-game days, I sold group outings, as everyone else did during their "spare time." We each were responsible for regions around Southtown in which to saturate with information regarding Guitars outings. I hated sales more than anything, and as the season started, I concentrated more on my concessions than on sales, and I failed to reach my sales goals. In fact, during one organizational meeting, the traveling general manager from Chicago called me out.

"So how are the Little League sales going?" the GM asked Todd, our new group sales director. Todd answered with some number short of our goal. The GM continued, "So what's up with that?" He turned to me, "What are you doing, Hakos?" I gave no response. I just thought, Are you fucking kidding me? What am I doing? What was I supposed to say? I worked non-stop organizing concessions, leaving little time for sales. I couldn't wait to get out of there.

In my quest to increase my sales, I ventured into someone's sales region, knowingly. When I arrived back at the office, Todd approached me.

"Why'd you go into Walley's region?" He was very stern, trying to play his role as director of sales.

"I didn't realize it was his zone."

Todd stared me down for a while. All I could think was, Oh, no. Not Todd too. Is this fuck trying to scold me? We looked at each other for a while, just standing there in the office with phones ringing and sales being pitched. I know we both didn't want to be in this situation. We both knew that the job was tearing at our souls. Later, on our balcony, we both apologized over a bottle of wine. We needed breaks.

We rarely enjoyed breaks during the season, but our schedule was set up so that we had a thirteen-day gap between home stands in July. I took this opportunity to take a break. I decided to arrange it so that the concessions would not have a delivery until two days before the next home stand. I spent the first couple days of this break cleaning what needed to be cleaned at the stadium. Then, I told everyone that I was taking a vacation. Lord knows I needed one. They hardly approved, but that didn't bother me. While everyone in the office continued selling tickets and running the daily affairs, I took a trip alone. I decided to drive eastward toward the Smokies. I went to my aunt and uncle's place in North Carolina and spent a night in their house up in the mountains. I continued on toward D.C., where my brother lived. From there, I drove to Akron. I enjoyed making frequent stops in the mountains. I had one conversation with a little girl who kept asking for more and more money.

"Can I have one of those white thingies?" she asked, holding her index finger and thumb a mere centimeter apart to show the size of the white thingie.

"A what?" I asked, quite confused.

"A little white thingie."

"A white thingie?"

"Yeah."

I picked up a dime. "You mean one of these?" I gave it to her.

"Maybe I could just have a dollar," she suggested.

"But I need the dollar." I said.

"One more."

I didn't understand her. "I have to go now."

"If you give me a dollar, I'll buy you a Coke."

I gave the kid a dollar, and she ran to get a soda. It seemed the only way to get rid of her so I could leave. I left before the girl could get back.

I continued my drive through the regal, rugged mountains. Many of my stops had signs that pointed to camp sites and hiking trails. The drive was a long one, but I enjoyed it. There I sat, refusing to turn the air on in my car. Instead, I basked in the relentless sun as the warm wind wiped across my car and into my opened windows. At each stop, my ears buzzed from the constant thunder of wind and radio. As grimy as rest stops are, I took pleasure in studying the everyday simplicities. I studied average people as they themselves made preparations for their drive across America. I inspected maps that led through lesser-traveled roads. Who knows what my goal was, but I do know that I enjoyed my solitude. Solitude? People surrounded me every moment of my trip. Vehicles filled with people raced past my aching BMW. As I imagined their agenda, I tried to figure where they were headed. Many people fought scrappy battles with their map, the folds playing tricks in the wind. The bathrooms I used along the way reeked of the waste from the person before me. The coffee that kept me awake on my trip was always handed to me by another human being, who barked at another human being next to them behind the counter. I wondered why this felt like solitude. Then it came to me: instead of being an integral character in this drive through America, I was merely a witness to the happenings going on around me. I was like Scrooge when he is led by the spirits, unable to be heard or touched. I was living a summer novel where I read about the characters but did not play along with them. This feeling of distance from my surroundings was a feeling of freedom. It was like listening to the news. I knew everything that was going on in the story, but I had no role to play—no effect. I only listened and observed. This was a relief from the life where I played such a huge role—top billing sucked.

I loved my vacation through the open country, but the taste of freedom only increased my disgust for the Guitars. Knowing that I had to go back to the life of top billing sickened me. My real life was like having every line in a four-hour one-act play—the stress was excruciating. I would rather just sit in the audience and watch.

Along the ride, I picked up my older brother in D.C. From there, we rode up through Pennsylvania toward Akron, Ohio. There's a mystery on this trip (beyond Breezewood). When nearing Pittsburgh, for what seems like hundreds of miles, signs pointing to Pittsburgh appear one after another. What look like millions of dead trees line the Pennsylvania Turnpike, creating a cartoon-like backdrop that never really changes. It makes it seem as though you are stuck in a time warp around Pittsburgh, never nearing it and never leaving it behind.

The mission for Nick and me was to attend the bachelor party of one of our childhood friends. The bachelor, Andrew, grew up with Nick. Andrew's brother Marty was my age. We planned to drive north to Cleveland and stay overnight at the Ritz-Carlton. From there, we would find our own unplanned fun.

For whatever reason, my brother and I thought that we should be nicely dressed for this occasion. We arrived at Andrew's house in coats and ties. Everybody laughed at us and wondered why we wore costumes. We marched into the bathroom and dressed down for our short journey up to Cleveland.

We checked into the Ritz and managed our way to the Great Lakes Brewing Company, a local brewpub. We chowed down and drank good beer. We stayed for what seemed like hours, drinking ourselves silly. We caught a cab and arrived at a nearby booby joint. Pretty high scale, the booby joint boomed with booby music and hypnotic lights. I grabbed another lap dance and gave the girl all my money. We left that booby joint and stumbled upon another. This booby joint reeked of second-class accommodations, but my brother and Andrew loved it. We poured hundreds of dollars into the panties of one dancer. Nick bought rounds of shots, and it was at this moment that he found nuptial clarity. After downing a fiery shot, he cleared his throat and leaned into Marty, nearly touching cheek to cheek.

"Marty," Nick struggled drunkenly, "would you do me the honor of being in my wedding in December?" Harsh alcohol breath bubbled around their heads like a wreath.

Surprised, given the scenario and setting, Marty uttered, "Yeah, um...sure."

Nick rolled his head back toward the breasts bouncing in front of him. Then, apparently bored with the disintegration of the night, he lost his temper with one of the booby chicks. After taking a smoke outside, he was barred from reentry. He stood solo outside, his finger in the face of a lady at the door. She refused to let him back inside. Irate, he lost his cool.

"You know how much money I've thrown into this place?" Nick said, heated. He kept his actions under control, but his face bunched with anger.

"I can't let you in unless you pay."

"You know what you're doing here...," my brother continued with stern comments and finger pointing.

The whole booby joint thing dragged. Several of us joined my brother outside and waited for the others. Soon after, someone came outside to collect more cash so that the personal dances could continue inside. We forked over the money and loitered around outside, kicking stones and telling stories.

Somehow, we found our way back to the Ritz. But Nick and Andrew were far from done. They got it in their heads that we should bring some dancers up to the room. They turned to the only person they knew in Cleveland, the cabby.

"Hey, Antonio, do you know of any girls?"

"What kind of girls?"

"Well you know...we don't want any funny business or sex or anything. We just want a show put on."

"Yeah, I know of some girls."

"Not any sex or anything."

"Yeah, I know of some."

"It can't be illegal or anything like that. We don't want any trouble."

"Don't worry. I got just the thing."

"Here is some money." Nick and Andrew scrounged around and compiled a crumpled handful of bills. They handed it to Antonio. Marty and I shook our heads, thinking the whole thing ridiculous.

"Now, you guys aren't cops, man," Antonio seriously said, assuring himself no problems.

"What?" Andrew blurted, confused at Antonio's comment. "No. It's not illegal. That's what we've been trying to say. If it's not illegal, then it doesn't matter if we're cops. But we're not."

Antonio drove off. We strolled back into the hotel. A few female stragglers of a wedding party floated around and reached the elevator at the same time as us. These two women had us by about 20 years, but Andrew found them attractive. However, the attempt to win them over failed miserably. In the name of safety, Andrew pleaded with the women that we were harmless.

"No. Now, really. It's not like we have a gun or anything. We're safe." Somehow, he thought this was an effective way to entice them to our room. He stumbled around the elevator with his fingers imitating a gun. His back hunched as he played the role. "Really, we're fine. You're totally safe with us. We have no guns or anything."

This appalled the women, who originally seemed like they might be interested. They got off the elevator and scampered away.

"Oh, yeah, like that was a way to pick up chicks," Marty and I said.

"Hey, I wanted them to know that they were safe," Andrew explained.

"Well, that's not the way to do it," said Marty.

We walked back to our room and awaited the call from Antonio. As we waited, our energy faded, and one by one, we fell asleep.

Suddenly, the hotel phone rang with its annoying hotel sound. I snapped from my sleep, quickly opening my eyes. I remained on the bed but saw Nick jump to his feet and answer the phone. The only other sound was the bellowing snores of sleepers with too much alcohol in their systems.

"Hello?" Nick said. "You know what, I think we're gonna have to pass on the girls tonight." He listened. "No. We're just not up to it right now." He listened. "You can just keep the money." Listened. "Nah, that's okay." Listened. "Okay, bye." My brother snuck back onto his bed through the sounds of deep snores. And that was that.

I woke early in the morning to hear bath water running. Apparently, feeling so awful, Andrew decided to take a warm bath. It was the only answer to his pain—the perfect irrational morning hangover reasoning. He dunked himself in the bath, and I fell back asleep.

I woke a little later. I decided to use some of the fantastic amenities of the Ritz. I didn't drink as much as some of the others, and I felt fine. I planned out a morning of swimming, hot tub, sauna and then breakfast. I walked down to the steam room and stepped into the foggy unknown. I felt around for a seat and sat down, wearing only a towel. To my surprise, a yogi sat not too far from me. The completely naked man looked to have a frail darkened body, but his face was round and smiley. His beard stretched down his navel.

"Are you from around here?" he asked in a high-pitched Indian accent.

"No. I'm from Southtown."

"Is it hot down there?"

"Not as hot as it is in here," I said, wiping my forehead. He giggled.

"Beautiful country," he said. The whole thing was a bit much for me after such a wild night. I decided to go.

"Well, that's enough for me." I walked out.

I got only a few steps away when the door opened behind me. "Too hot for you!" the yogi screeched and giggled, as I smiled and continued on my way.

I rode the elevator back up to the room and dressed for breakfast. Marty and I reached breakfast and found Andrew sitting slumped over in a small chair across from one of his friends. Andrew seemed to be nursing some juice as his friend comforted him. Marty and I took to the buffet, which included a delightful array of foods. We stacked our plates, but ate very little. Our stomachs wouldn't allow much. After that, we quietly sat in the car on our way back to Akron. And that's how bachelor parties go.

25 BRUTAL MISERY

Back in Southtown, my anger increased. A Saturday afternoon game, the blue sky allowed the sun to shine fully, beautifying life more than usual. Fans squinted as they relaxed in their plastic stadium seating. Their feet propped up against the chair backs in front of them, sipping at their cold beers, exerting no energy, allowing themselves to soak in the joys of life. I pitifully stared at these fans, wishing I could be sitting in their places, drinking a beer. I looked to the sun. He smiled at me; I frowned back at him. All this was so unfair. How can I work on a Saturday afternoon, while all these people enjoy themselves? What misery. What torture. My blood rose. I wiped my forehead, smearing the sweat across my face. I took a moment and moved on with my job. All I needed now was for some asshole employee to get in my way. Soon, someone would feel my anger.

In these moments, any employee who I thought a punk got yelled at. Sometimes I lost my mind completely. Like the time the kid refused to go to the stand I told him to because he moaned of being tired. He sat, snubbing me over and over again as I screamed at him.

"You think you're a fuckin' tough ass? You're only sixteen-years old! You don't fuckin' know shit!" I blasted into this young punk. I felt exhausted and really wanted nothing to do with laziness. I bitched this sixteen-year old back into his mama's womb. He walked straight to the telephone when I was done with him and called his mama. His dad showed up, and I got a call to go to the office. This punk's dad told me straight. Here I was, bitching at a kid. This abuse was completely uncalled for, not to mention probably illegal, especially when I used "fuck" every other word.

Dad was setting me straight. "Now I could press charges on you and this entire organization." I stood listening, exhibiting a facial expression that denoted disappointment of my actions. "I won't do that though. Instead, I want you two to shake hands and make up. I realize these kids are sometimes hard to control, and they got a mind of their own, but you can't treat them how you did." The reamed-out employee and I shook hands, and we went back to work. I'll never forget the patience and impact of dad's words.

Yelling at employees was not the way to take out my aggression. I needed something else. Cash registers. The registers in the stands always acted up—not opening, not turning on, not adding correctly, not showing any numbers. The registers always gave me a problem. The most frustrating was when there was a line ten people deep waiting to get up to the front to order so they could go back in the sticky heat and watch the game. People get very irritated when waiting. But the worst was when the register with ten people waiting breaks. Then there is serious griping, and I am the one who takes the brunt of the whining when I come and fix the register. During one sold-out game, my registers malfunctioned at levels not even the most clever register technician could solve. I ran into stand three and quickly reprogrammed an unused register and placed it in the spot of the register that was not working. Of course, since I changed registers on him in the middle of the game, this employee's register would never balance, meaning that the entire stand balance sheet would be a mess, but when the fans start getting restless, all formalities go out the window. I fixed the problem in stand three and ran over to stand four.

"What the hell?" When I entered, two employees sat on the freezer eating ice cream from a miniature baseball helmet. I turned to the stand manager, "What are they doing?"

"Well they can't do nothin' with their register's out."

I turned to the ice cream buddies, "Get rid of the ice cream and clean up."

They looked at me like I was crazy to want them to look presentable. They both asked, "Why?"

"Cuz!" I shouted and turned my concentration to the register. I fixed the register tape in about four seconds, looked back at the kids sitting on the freezer with ice cream on their face, and ran out to check on my group of Lutherans at their picnic.

Being in charge of Little League sales and church outings, I frequently needed to welcome my groups during the game. The Lutherans, the smallest of the church groups, traditionally brought about eighty people to the game. But being the smallest didn't mean they were going to have the least fun. The Lutherans also traditionally tailgated in the parking lot before the game, drinkin' and eatin' and havin' a good ole time. I got along well with the outing organizer, so I ran out of the stadium and into the parking lot to meet Bob the Lutheran.

"Hey, Hakos," he greeted.

"Hey, Bob."

He introduced me to his wife and a few who stood around him.

"Well, I gotta get back," I said.

"Of course, it looks like you're pretty busy."

"A little."

"A little?" he laughed. I ran back inside the stadium high walls.

While discretely plowing my way through meandering fans in the concourse, I noticed a little boy who spilled his nachos on the ground.

"Justin!" His mom yelled.

I ran straight into the nearest stand and grabbed some nachos. "Put this on your employee comp list," I quickly said to the stand manager. I ran out toward the boy who was still standing there, mystified with his hands held out as if he were praying to the heavens. His mom wiped the cheese from the child's shirt, scolding him.

"Here." I handed the boy some more nachos. The mom looked up at me surprised. The boy began to eat his new nachos.

"Thank you," The mom said, "Say thank you to the man, Justin." The boy just kept eating.

"That's ok." I ran off for stand one.

When I ran past stand three, I heard someone shouting for me, "Hakos!" It was the stand three manager, my friend Peter, so I stopped.

"Yeah?" I asked.

"I can't get the Bud tapped."

Usually, I hung out with Peter for a little bit, but I was kind of pissy at this point. I rushed into stand three's cooler and located the untapped keg. There was already beer on the ground from when Peter tried to tap it. I tried once to hook the hose up, but since the hose was jammed in the open position, the beer sprayed everywhere when I attempted to tap the keg. I tried to unjam the hose, but I couldn't. To save time, I turned my head and shoved the hose on the keg. For a few seconds, beer sprayed everywhere again, including on me. I slammed the connection down, tapping the keg; I exited the cooler, and told my friend that he was all set. Later, Peter told me how funny it looked to see me walk out, drenched in beer, but for me, it was hardly funny.

I ran out of stand three, told a couple of employees to stand up, and reached stand one.

"Hakos, where have you been?" the stand manager asked impatiently. She had been dealing with angry customers on her own.

I looked up over her counter at the crowd forming in the lines. They jittered and crept about like little possessed trolls. They barked and snapped at each other. These unhappy fans boiled within. It seemed only time before they demonically transform, like a werewolf during a full moon.

I took the broken register aside and started working on it. I finally got the drawer opened, and inside the drawer, I found a pool of water.

"What the fuck?" I looked at it for a second, confused. I scanned the panting fans. At that moment, the radio disrupted me again. It was Brad's voice saying, "Plastic Patty," an emergency code that meant there was a problem at Hitler. I ignored the radio for a moment, and in my rage, I picked up the register and threw it in the trashcan next to me. I turned to the manager and said, "You only got three registers now." I ran out of the stand and headed for Hitler.

As I quickly made my way toward the grill, I could see a cloud of smoke above the field. It came from Hitler, and it slowly floated across the field. When I saw it, the smoke had just reached the pitcher's mound. Just then, I got a call on the radio.

"Hakos?"

"Yeah?"

"Plastic Patty!"

I ran down to the grill area. Anybody who worked at the grill received my greatest sympathy and attention. Earlier in the season, we established the Order of Grillbilly. Anybody working at the grill was a Grillbilly. Together, we helped each other out and worked our asses into the ground. Brad headed Hitler and the cooking of the food. He was experiencing the same shit I went through the past two years; however, nobody really knew how to tame Hitler like I could, meaning that Brad frequently called me down to the grill to fix any problems.

I reached Hitler. Smoke charged out from inside the diabolical beast. Grease fire! I saw Brad fighting a deranged grease fire. He stood on the side of Hitler with one of the side panels open. Fire gushed from the opening, causing Brad to duck below it. I ran to help him.

"I got this," he said, "The turning belt broke." I ran into the room next door and pulled a large nail from a cup of many large nails. It was our emergency stock. While grabbing a nail I got a call on the radio.

"Hakos?"

"Yeah?"

"I got two guys freed up from the picnics. Where do you want them?" The picnics were ending, and picnic guys were sending up the workers they didn't need any more. I knew stand four was having problems scooping ice cream so I suggested they go there.

"Hakos, I don't need those workers," said the stand manager from stand four.

"Ok. Send them to stand two." This was the largest stand, and it was the only other place I could think of that needed help. I knew I couldn't send kids home yet; it was too early in the game.

"Ok, Hakos."

I ran back to the grill and stuck the nail into the hole so that the turning belt would catch and begin rotating the racks again. When I finished that, I opened the lid of Hitler, and I began taking off the racks that had been singed by the grease fire.

"We're getting slammed," Brad confessed.

"Yeah, I know."

"Can you have FDR do those dogs there?" FDR was the new convection oven that the team purchased so that we could better handle the crowds of ten or twelve thousand.

"Yeah, no problem." I selected a runner, and together the runner and I ran ten cases of dogs around the back of the home run fence all the way to the third base side. FDR was situated in a newly furnished kitchen just behind the team dugout. I ran in and gave the griller the new dogs.

"Do you have any cooked dogs to take up to the stands?"

"Yeah, those there."

I picked up a tray of about one hundred dogs, told the runner to go back to Hitler, and I ran the cooked dogs up to stand three. On my way, I got a call that stand two needed dogs. I ran into stand two, and I gave them half of my dogs. The stand was a mess. There was no time to clean the stands with such an onslaught of hungry fans. I watched briefly as workers ran back and forth from the registers to the prep tables, creating a blurred vision of absolute chaos. Then I ran to stand three to deliver the other half, but not before getting two more calls for dogs.

"Brad, do you have those dogs or should I have FDR do those?" I called on the radio. I wondered if Brad had caught up in his cooking yet.

"Yeah, I got about two hundred ready. Should I split 'um up between the stands?"

"Yeah."

Just then, another call, "Hakos, can I see you at stand six?"

I hated stand six. Everything to do with stand six sucked. I only opened it when I really needed to, and this game really needed it. While I ran to stand six, I got a call from the guy who ran the little pizza stand that sat across from stand three.

"Hakos, I need five more pepperonis and five more cheese."

I nodded and grabbed my radio again, "Brad?"

"I got it." Brad answered. Brad kept the pizzas in the freezer by Hitler. The Guitars had taken it upon themselves to cook their own pizzas, rather than bring in a company as we did in the past. I needed Brad to send a runner up with the pizzas; luckily, he could spare someone. When I entered stand six, I saw the manager standing there with two cups of foam.

"This is what's coming out of the taps."

Actually, that's what always came out of the taps in stand six. I just hoped that it wouldn't happen this time, but it did.

"Fuck it. You don't sell beer." I said.

"Don't serve beer?"

"Nah, your taps are all fucked. Fuck it."

"Ok. That'll make it easier."

I called vending and had them send a beer portable to the area outside stand six. I quickly got the vendor who was to work the portable a bank and stocked her with beer. I figured this could take the beer business for stand six.

I left the vendor and headed for Mel Belle's Backyard Grill. The Backyard Grill cooked fresh product over a real charcoal grill about the length of four trash barrels. It was a big hit with the fans. I hadn't checked Mel for a while so I thought I would pay him a visit. Earlier in the year, we arranged Mel's grill across from stand one, so I ran back to the other side of the stadium. The line at the Backyard Grill resembled the lines at newly opened roller coasters at amusement parks. Mel labored over the hot coals, cooking burgers, chicken, brats (or bracs, as Mel would say), and many other labor-intensive items.

"Mel, how's it going?"

"Fine." Mel was always fine. He wasn't a very good meter for how things were going.

I checked everything out, and I walked up to Shikera, who was serving. She had worked at the stadium for a while, and she and I had a good relationship. She was older and had a good head on her shoulders.

"Shikera, how's it going?"

"Fine. I mean, we got a long line, but we doin' fine with food. We ok."

"Cool. Thanks."

"Yeah."

Again, I was off and running. I ran past the pizza guy, who yelled out for his ten pizzas.

"Coming," I yelled back and kept running. It was nearing the seventh inning stretch. Most everything was under control, and Brad and I asked earlier to sing "Take Me Out to the Ballgame." I reached Hitler and asked Brad if he was ready. I called over to FDR to see if he could handle things for a while. Things were slowing down anyway, so I thought everything would be fine.

The announcer introduced us as the concessions staff. Brad and I marched out to the field, and together we sloppily sang that most famous baseball song. It was a wonderful release from the earlier rush of events.

Finally, the game ended, and the concessions crew filed into our office and began the long and tedious job of counting out and balancing the stands. First off, the stands never balanced completely. Sometimes we were over by a couple hundred. Sometimes we were under by a thousand. After mathematically figuring that we were off, we had to determine why, which usually meant me joining the stand manager for a recount of the stand. We counted cups, chips, peanuts, popcorn containers, nacho plates, beer cups, foil pans, and candy. We did this in the late hours of the night. Sometimes we found the problem. Other times we couldn't figure it out. Sometimes we blamed certain employees whose register was off by hundreds of dollars, and sometimes we just said, "Fuck it."

Before walking down to recount stand two, my superior told me that the beer vendor I set up across from stand six had been caught selling to an under-aged kid. She thought the kid was of age; he showed her an ID. It just so happened that an undercover official was at the game, and he caught the illegal sale. This was just another tiring complication. Later, we went to court. While sitting in court with my employee, I got to see other cases go before us. One attorney caught my attention. He wore an earring and long hair. He attempted, quite smoothly, to help one of his clients, but the client refused to cooperate.

"Would you just calm the fuck down!" the attorney yelled. "I've gotten your brother out of jail! Your mother out! I've gotten your whole fuckin' family out of jail! So, you better show me some respect! Now sit the fuck down and shut up!"

"Wow," I thought. Impressive. I never knew courtrooms worked like that. "Crazy." In the end, I merely sat there taking notes. I felt bad for my employee. She was an older lady, making very little money. Why would anybody want to take her down? She didn't know the kid was under age. Finally, my employee got some nonsensical probation. Pointless.

Back at the stadium, I was in the process of examining stand two's balance sheet, when all of a sudden a strange voice came over the radio.

"Hey, Hakos. I'm gonna get you, mother fucker." We all looked up at each other confused.

"Who was that?" someone asked.

"Dunno," I shrugged it off and continued counting.

"I gotcho radio, and I'm gonna get you, mother fucker." The voice again talked. Apparently, one of the employees stole a radio, and now he was harassing us. He spoke about many people in the front office of how he was going to "get them."

"I check out your booty Jamie. Yeah."

"Who is that?" Someone from the front office talked back over the radio.

"I'm the nigga whose gonna getcha."

"We'll find you."

The voice merely laughed this time into the radio. I attempted to shrug it off, but some people would not let it go. One person cursed back at the radio. I thought that was useless. All of a sudden, people from the staff were searching the stadium grounds. I finished my counting and decided to get involved too. Why the hell not? I thought it was certain that the kid was not in the stadium. Instead, he was talking to us from outside the stadium, so I wandered outside into the neighborhoods.

"I see you, Hakos," the ominous voice whispered. I wasn't sure if he was just fucking with me or what, but I made sure to be careful, as careful as I could in the Southtown Hood.

I circled the stadium as far as I could. When I reached the street, a car pulled up to me. It was Todd. "Hakos, what the hell are you doing out here?"

"I thought I'd look for the kid."

Todd laughed, "You better have a gun."

"I have this lighter."

We both laughed, "Yeah, that'll help you, Hakos." Todd drove off.

I started looking around at my surroundings—an abandoned building and parking lot to one side and a desolate road to the other. The clouds quickly passed by the bright moon. What the fuck am I doing? I gave up on the search and headed back for the stadium. It was the end of a home stand. What the fuck did I care about a damn radio. Last time I spent time looking for a radio, the person who took it died. I jumped into my car to meet some of my coworker friends at Taco Company. I drove with the warm air blowing on my sweaty face and arm. I felt tired from the ridiculous intensity of the night. Every game raced this way, dealing me a wild hand, knocking me around like a rag doll. I took each beating and somehow broke the riddle of each game like a cowboy breaks a restless stallion.

When I arrived at Taco Company, the bucket-o-beers had already been ordered. I sat down and quickly opened a Rolling Rock.

"You made it," Todd said.

"Yeah," I replied.

"Did you find him?"

"Nah. I just walked around the neighborhood like an idiot."

"Yeah. That was pretty stupid."

"Yeah."

"Well, I had some winners down in the picnics today," Todd began his story.

"That whole stadium is filled with winners," commented Johnny, another concessions loser.

"Ha. No shit," agreed another.

"What happened?" I asked.

"Oh, nothing. Just a fuck who thought he deserved everything." Todd threw his hands in the air. Todd worked as the director of sales, but his game-time duty consisted of preparing and setting up picnics. He continued his story about a client of his who booked a picnic. "He comes up to me in the middle of the picnic and asks where the chicken is. I'm like, 'You didn't pick the menu with the chicken on it.' And he says, 'But they have chicken.' He's pointing to this other picnic. 'Well, they bought the package with the chicken.' The guy couldn't understand it. Dumbass." We all shook our heads, understanding Todd's troubles with a world filled with dumbasses.

"Oh, but this one's better," Todd continued. "The best one is when we were setting up for the picnic. You know, we were so packed today; we didn't have time to do shit. Well, it was like five minutes before the gates had opened, and I'm putting the barbeque in the steam table. Well, you know those aluminum pans are so flimsy. Well, I'm fightin' this barbeque, you know, tryin' to get it in, when it falls into the steam table." There was a universal "Oooh" from the listeners. "Well, you know what's in the water in the steam table. We didn't have time to wash it today. You know, we were so busy, and it's the last game of the home stand, so there's like bugs and dirt and pasta from five games ago in there. Well, this barbeque drops right in this shit. Well I just said, 'Fuck it,' I don't have time for this shit. I just lifted the barbeque back up and got it back into place." We all laughed. We had all been in that position before where the need to be prompt beat out morals. Todd carried on, "I turn, and see one of our quality picnic staffers had seen the whole thing. So I turned to him and said, 'You saw nothing.'"

"Was that the picnic of the guy who wanted the chicken?" Johnny asked.

Todd thought a moment and then said, "Yeah, I think it was."

"Serves the bastard right," I added.

I reached across the table and cracked open my third Rolling Rock as Peter began his story about me tapping the keg in concession stand three. He followed up that story with another.

"You know, I'll never understand how some of the trash gets the way it does. Tonight, I was picking up trash, and I bend over to pick up a regular uneaten tray of nachos, and I go to pick it up, but it like pulls back. I'm thinking, now this isn't right. This is just a regular tray of nachos. It should pick up. All the other trays of nachos pick up. So I tried again, and it still pulled back. So I get down on my hands and knees, and I peer through the seat to see why it won't lift, you know. I lifted up the tray just a little, and I noticed that there was gum lining the entire tray. Not just a stick or two of bubble gum, this was like the whole pack, cementing the tray to the ground. Now, I'm thinking, did the people put the gum on the tray or the ground first, and did they plot this gumming?" We cracked up while Peter imitated the fan who did the gumming, "Last time I went to a game, my nacho tray got kicked over. I won't let that happen again. I've got the perfect plan. I'm going to partially chew a whole pack of gum, stick it on the bottom of the nacho tray, and then stick the tray to the ground. Yeah, that should work."

Peter's trash story got us on a trash-talking spree. Peter remembered the time we used the truck to pick up trash in the parking lot. "We thought we had gotten everything, until Brad noticed a piece of trash down the hill. I think Ken was driving, and so he headed for the trash. They were trying to be all slick with the whole thing."

"Yeah, slick with trash," I added.

"Yeah." Peter laughed and continued, "So Ken is lining this trash up so Brad could just scoop it up on the other side by dropping his hand to the parking lot. And they're getting close, and everyone in the truck is cheering, and

Sweaty Mascots start Grease Fires

Ken lines up the trash perfectly, and Brad makes a perfect scoop, and he pulls it into the truck, and then they notice that it's a dirty diaper, and everyone's like, 'Ahhh, nooooo, a dirty diaper!'"

The whole crew laughed, and then Todd and I invited everyone to our apartment for the weekend for a keg of Heineken. How did we get the Heineken? Well, one of Todd's clients ordered a keg of Heineken for their picnic, and they barely touched it. Knowing this and being in charge of the concessions, I knew we could borrow the keg for a while, finish it and bring it back. The Covert Heineken Mission needed a third person, Johnny. The three of us, Johnny, Todd and me, waited for the right moment and then carried out our plan. Todd and I ran down to concession stand two, where the Heineken sat in a cold cooler. Johnny ran to his truck and carefully pulled it down in to the concourse. Johnny backed his truck bed up to the door of stand two, and Todd and I hoisted the keg into the truck. We covered it with a sheet, and Johnny casually drove away. Later, we sped the truck off to our apartment, and we carefully placed the keg into a trashcan of ice on our balcony.

That weekend we sat out on our balcony and drank Heineken, even when we didn't want to. Johnny and Ken came over, and they helped us out a little. We got bit by this obsession to knock out the security light that shined from above our balcony. Todd claimed he was going to shoot it. He walked inside and brought out a gun.

"What the fuck are you gonna do with that?" asked Johnny.

"I'm gonna shoot out that fuckin' light," Todd responded.

Johnny laughed, but I didn't find too much humor in the whole episode since I lived there.

"Don't shoot it man. Just don't do it," I pleaded.

"I'm sick of this light? What's the use of it?" Todd questioned.

"Who cares just let it go," I insisted, while the rest laughed.

"It's right above the people who live above you. What if you miss and shoot them?" Johnny asked, laughing.

"I don't care. I won't miss, though." Todd aimed for a long time, checking his composure and examining his angle. His body shifted back and forth with Heineken. He got close to shooting, but after a concentrated effort from the rest of us to let the light go, Todd backed down.

I snuck into my room early on the first night of the keg and went to sleep. Outside I could hear the guys shouting and laughing. I'm sure they enjoyed the night, but I felt so drunk with comfort in my bed that I didn't care.

26 A POSSIBLE ESCAPE PLAN

I woke up early the next morning and drove to my favorite coffee joint in Southtown, Sparky. Every morning before work, I stopped in at Sparky and ordered the usual. Some of the employees knew me by name and by drink. The whole place felt very comfortable to me. I stood in line and waited to order. A little kid in front of me wore his Southtown Guitars hat, and he and his dad talked about the game the night before. They mentioned this hit and that hit and this player and that player. They even mentioned the smoke that slowly drifted across the field. They talked so excitedly about their time at the park, I hated it. Little did they know that behind that smoke was a grill named Hitler. They had no clue that I was responsible for the ordering and cooking of their food at the stadium. Baseball is definitely not a glamorous job, but I was never really looking for any recognition in my work from the fans or the staff. Or maybe I was. Why was I working in this crummy job? Or maybe the job was fine and I was crummy. Either way, I didn't fit the job. I loved everything outside of work but not my work. Why live my life in this fashion? I thought there must to be a way to enjoy both my work and free time. The little boy looked up at me. I smiled at him and he smiled back. That was all I was looking for, a nice smile.

I reached the counter. The guy behind the counter recognized me. He smiled and asked if I wanted the regular. I told him yes and included some oatmeal. I got my oatmeal and deeply caffeinated drink and sat down by the window in the morning sun. I picked up a paper and quickly tossed out the sports page. I turned to the front page and read some headlines that looked interesting. I spotted a movie in the paper that I wanted to see. I decided to hang out at Sparky for a while before going to the movie.

I had some time before the movie after finishing breakfast. I drove to a park in Southtown that boasted a lovely open space for picnicking, as well as many large trees and a stream that emptied out into a little pool. I walked around the park and watched the geese mope around. I checked out a bum who slept under a bridge. I didn't get too close to him, but I watched him from afar. Scattered wrappers of eaten food were blowing about him. It was warm outside, but he wore layers of clothes. However, he looked very peaceful in his sleep. I wondered if it was better to hate your job or have no job at all. I couldn't make up my mind, and I pressed on through the park. My dad's words "what are you doing" repeated in my head as I looked up at the trees and the birds. I couldn't answer the question. It was not that I was in dire need of some psychological counseling or anything like that; rather, I just hated my current state, and I struggled with what to do.

After about an hour of walking, I drove to the theater where I stayed for a couple of hours. Following the movie, I felt satisfied with the amount of time I spent alone. I called Todd who met me back at Sparky. Together we came to the decision to taste test as many double mochas as we could. We started at Sparky, and then we headed down the main drag of Southtown toward downtown. We drank our mocha along the way and talked about funny happenings at this place and that place. We talked about the time we accidentally found some opened doors at the university late at night. We entered the building and walked around the halls and the classrooms. We wrote messages on the chalkboards and threw staplers out the windows. We turned on some projectors and then quietly left. We talked about the time Butch attempted to jump out of a bar window to catch some girl. Unfortunately, he wore these new cowboy boots that got caught on the railing. He landed on the pavement with a smack and got up and limped away. We also began to talk about sending out resumes to different teams. Todd was ready to move. He was originally from Oregon, and the move to Southtown was too far. He claimed he was happy to have made the move, but he wanted to head back to the Northwest. We decided to make a team effort in building a spreadsheet with as many minor league teams and addresses as possible. We would turn this into a giant mailer of cover letters and resumes. We would use free time at the stadium to put this together. Both of us had lost our care for being the greatest employee in the world. Truthfully, both of us could have done our job without thinking or without much effort. We knew the job perfectly. We decided to use envelopes from the stadium and the mailing machine to stamp the postage. The Guitars were going to pay for our giant mailer. It was a great plan. We had found our ticket out of Southtown.

We arrived at another coffee place and bought another mocha. At this particular joint, we found it customary to help ourselves to a bag of chocolate covered espresso beans. One of us usually took a bag as the girl steamed our beverages. We bought one more mocha before heading back to our cars. On our way, we eyed a trashcan. It was a hefty, industrial trashcan with a sturdy, metal lid.

"Why don't we take that lid?" Todd suggested.

"Why?"

"I don't know. To remember Southtown by?"

"Ok."

I think the mochas corrupted our easily manipulative, 20-something logic. We covertly moseyed around the trashcan until the right moment presented itself. Then, together we lifted the lid, which was heavier than we thought.

"Go!" Todd screamed.

"My spleen! I think I popped it!" I shouted.

We began running down the street with the lid. We cared little for the cars, but we tried to avoid people. We hid behind a couple of trees during our getaway to evade passersby. After a long jaunt, we reached Todd's car. We threw the trashcan lid in the back of his car, and then we fell over laughing.

"That was the stupidest thing ever," I laughed out.

"I know! But that's what made it so great, Hakos!"

"What the hell. Why did we do that?" We both laughed for a while. "Oh, fuck it. I'll see you back home for a Heineken."

Todd left, and I walked to my car, which I parked in a lot across the street. When I reached my car, I heard some rumbling. I turned and saw a man crawling out of a dumpster. I couldn't move; I had to watch. He stumbled over to me.

"Hey man," the man from the dumpster said. He had definitely been drinking, and he looked broken down. His beard was crusted with some junk on it, and his clothes looked just as scrappy. He spoke with a strong slur, and he smelled like mustard.

"Hello," I answered.

"Hey man, I'm not feeling so hot. How are you?" He reached out his hand to shake. I put out my hand, and when our hands touched, I felt a squish between them. I looked down at our hands, and a yellowish ooze spewed out between them. My stomach churned.

"Hey man. I don't know what to do," he said as he placed his hand on my car.

"What do you mean?"

"I lost everything man. I lost my wife and my job. I got nothing. And I gave all of my money to my son so he could go to college." I began to forget about the yellow ooze in my hand. "I did the right thing didn't I man?" His shadowy wrinkles presented a sorry soul.

"Yeah, of course. You gave your son money so he could go to school. That's the right thing."

"Did I do the right thing?" the man was in a stupor. He often turned his head to the left as if to refocus his eyes. Then he looked back at me with a stare while his head seemed to float above his neck with a sort of bobble.

"Yeah, you did the right thing." I started to get a little nervous.

"I had a great executive job. Then my wife died in a car accident. That hurt me man. I went to some psycho guy, but I couldn't cope man. I lost my job and gave my money to my son. That was the right thing, right?"

"Yeah. That was good."

"I thought so. I thought so." Just as I thought the Mustard Man was satisfied, he repeated his question, "That was good, right?"

"Yeah."

This went on for a while. Finally, the Mustard Man decided to leave. I shook his hand again. I figured my hand was already corroding from the earlier handshake. Then, the Mustard Man disappeared back into the dumpster. My problem about work and life looked so insignificant after my nonsense conversation with Mustard Man.

I ran back to Sparky, washed my hands, ran back to my car, gagged at the markings left by Mustard Man's hand on my car, jumped into my car, and drove home. I thought for a moment on my way home. I thought of nothing in particular, in fact I thought quite blankly. My brain found it difficult to process the emotions stirred by the Mustard Man. Mustard Man faded into the deeper parts of my brain, and I thought again of my job and myself. I thought that there must be something more out there. More than baseball. More than feeling frustrated. More than the everyday gloom.

I met Todd at home. He already sat with beer in hand, slurping on the Heineken. I told him about the Mustard

Man, and he reminded me that there was a trashcan lid in his car. We laughed, and then broke our code about talking about work at home. We revived our conversation about the mass mailing of resumes and smiled from the vision of foreseen victory.

While analyzing our plan, we brainstormed ideas about when to conduct the actual mailing. It was easy to stay after work past the hour when anybody else would be there. Todd and I usually met in the team weight room after 5:30 p.m. to work out. Afterwards, we jogged around a nearby Civil War fort. By the time we were through, nobody else was around. On our way out of the stadium, we locked the front gate. Early in the morning, I, being the first to arrive, opened the front gate. With this in mind, Todd and I organized a flawless master plan: We would partake in our usual workout ritual; however, instead of locking the gate on the way out, we would lock the gate and stay in the walls of the stadium, allowing us free access to the office facilities.

I envisioned scenes from black and white movies of close-up printing presses hard at work. Though, instead of filing out the daily headlines, this picture's close-up shots would be of printed resumes and envelope after envelope of stamped requests for employment. It was quite an image.

The night dragged on, and Todd and I continued our conversation. We exhausted the topic of the mass mailing. The subjects of old stories and girls took the floor. Our friend Ken soon joined Todd and me on the back balcony. Together we sipped wine and beer. I made sure not to inhale when bringing the glass to my mouth for the scent of the Mustard Man still rested in the pores of my hand. Todd and I joyfully changed the topic to that of women: What is the best part of the woman. We each took our turn in supporting our thesis. Ken claimed that the lips were the most inspiring part. Todd argued that the hair was certainly the most crucial element. He couldn't see himself falling in love with a woman who couldn't even keep her hair in check. I, on the other hand, demanded the importance of a woman's eyes. This feature, I believed, made everything. A girl could have the perfect high cheekbones and the most necessarily angled chin, but if the eyes did not match the rest, there was no need to list the girl on the list of "must-haves."

We ended our night in a stalemate, and I went to sleep, awaking with the chilled feeling of going back to work.

Each time I thought of leaving the Guitars, I got that wonderful feeling of pure happiness. I came to the decision to leave the Guitars whether I found a new job or not. I wanted to move closer to Akron, but I refused to restrict myself. I wanted to leave all my options opened and avoid any situation like the current. The entire Guitars future was in turmoil.

Disruptions in the ownership and front office marred my third season with the Guitars. After Al left, the owner placed the general manager from our sister team in Chicago in charge of us. He flew back and forth, from city to city, expecting that a few days a week in Southtown could keep things in order. After a while, he quit coming down to Southtown, and the team ran without a general manager for most of the season. As the season progressed, more and more decisions were being made by an unknown phantom figure who worked for the owner. Many of the usual workings began to change. We no longer picked up trash after the games; we no longer got reimbursed for miles we drove when conducting sales; and a stricter count of the inventory was kept by a new crew of interns whose direct superior was the Phantom. Personally, it annoyed me to be questioned by an intern who had only just arrived. I began referring to the interns as Mutant Interns. Each employee became more disgruntled as more and more new measures were passed without our consent. The fact that these decisions were being made by someone who had never worked in baseball worsened the feelings within the organization. With worsening attitudes in the front office came worsening interoffice relationships. The office separated to the point that everybody ran their own department, flushing everyday working conditions down the toilet. This was no clean flush; it was so ugly that it left muddy streaks all the way down the toilet bowl.

We had become familiar and comfortable with the way Al had run things. The old crew was a hard-nosed staff that got its hands dirty. This philosophy set us at odds with the Phantom. The new people were cleaner, wimpier number crunchers who couldn't understand our military-like ways. We began to see that the owner was merely waiting this season out in order to get to the off-season, where things could be done in the fashion of the phantom decision maker. We believed there was going to be a shake-up in the office, and we later found ourselves to be right.

This excruciating shake-up with the Guitars pushed me to write a series of short comic books dealing with the horrors. In the books, the concessions crew fought a losing battle against the Mutant Interns. The Phantom who led the Mutant Interns held too much power for the lowly Grillbillies. Through a series of several ridiculous turn of events, the Grillbilly order died out. In the end, a large-scale battle between the Phantom's Mutant Interns and the Grillbillies left the whole state of affairs in ruins. The entire Guitars organization fell into chaos, and the Phantom lived out his last days as a bag boy at a grocery store.

I could not have cared less about the change of direction on the large scale of the team. I only saw how the changes disrupted my daily responsibilities. Though the fact that I was entering my last weeks as a Guitar felt good, I still had a whole series of home stands to deal with. One way to deal with my torture at the Guitars was to take it out on the truck. The truck had been with us from nearly the beginning, an original member. There was a previous green truck, but he died and was sitting in the far distance of the parking lot of the stadium, decaying away. The current truck was kind of my best friend at the stadium. I didn't have a dog, but I had the truck. Together, we loaded cases of food and beverages, and we even got into a little trouble. Near the beginning of the season, I was backing up through the main gate. The driver's side door swung open and caught the side of the gate. I had my head turned to look where I was going, and, by the time I saw the disaster coming, it was too late. The gate crunched the door backwards. I spent several minutes trying to shove the door back into place, but it was useless. I cut the fuses to all the indoor lights, because they stayed on if the door was opened. At first, I was a little scared, but later I kind of laughed about it with my superior and concessions bum, Johnny.

Later, we took off the door just to make things easier. This became the start of an ongoing dismantling of the truck. Johnny took off the other door. This made things fun. We could just jump into the truck and be on our way without opening or closing anything. Later, I backed up with the bed door down, and I smashed that all up. It became our mission to see how much the truck could take. By the end, the entire dash was removed, and Todd smashed out the back window—it was great. For the final hurrah on the truck, my Grillbilly intern and I hot-rodded the truck around the parking lot. We peeled out and sprayed gravel through the thick Southtown air. We pulled Bullit-like moves and other car stunts only seen in the movies. The glorious climax revealed itself in the image of the old green truck. It was just sitting there so lonely. We decided to put the green truck out of his misery. We positioned our truck at one end of the lot, facing the green truck. We revved up our engine, set the wheels in motion with my foot on the brake, and took off straight ahead. Dust and dirt flew from our pure speed. The rocky surface of the parking lot made it difficult to control. Our tail swayed back and forth from the power, but we stayed the course. We headed closer, and I wondered what the crash would bring. We rammed into the green truck. I heard crunches of metal and glass shattering. We cheered in hollers just like a couple of good 'ole boys. We did it a couple more times. All the while, I giggled and shouted for joy. I had lost my mind. We hopped out of the truck and gave it a good patting.

"Good old truck," I said, "It's like my horse. I'm gonna have to brush him and clean out the dirt from his tires." I obsessed myself with doing strange things to counter my feelings for the real work.

After we finished playing Dukes of Hazard in the parking lot, a delivery truck pulled up to the front gate. Johnny and I hopped back into the truck and sped off toward the delivery truck. I brought our truck to a screeching halt by the back of the delivery truck.

"Hey, man, wassup?" I asked the delivery driver.

He handed me an invoice. It was a small delivery, little spur of the moment type stuff. Johnny and I unloaded the truck as we spoke bullshit with the delivery driver.

"How are things goin'?" I asked the driver.

"Oh, I don't know, man. I've been going nonstop since five this mornin'," he replied.

"Damn. You gotta take a rest, man," I suggested.

"Can't. Need the money. I tell you what, Hakos. They got me bustin' my ass nonstop, but I need it."

"Know what ya mean, man."

"I gotta a little girl who's in camp right now, and I got a boy playing baseball. Once I finish this shit, I gotta go watch the boy's game."

"Damn. You got no time for yourself."

"Nah. Watchin' my boy is great. You should see these kids out there messin' around. They haven't a clue; neither does the coach. I might could coach better than that idiot."

"Fuck the idiot," I said.

We finished loading up the truck.

"That's it, Hakos."

"That was nothing." I signed the invoice. "Hey, let me ask ya something. How do you do it? I mean, how do you work like you do and still have the patience to sit with your family?"

"Tough, Hakos. Tough. But, it's just what I do now. That's my life."

"Damn. See ya later." Johnny and I sent off the delivery driver with a wave, and then the two of us drove the truck down into the concourse area, where we met Short Dog.

"Hey, Short Dog," I said.

"Watsup, Hakos." Short Dog was short—almost a midget—a black man who we hired to clean the concession stands and chop up some vegetables for the restaurant. He was a shady character, but he worked hard. He also brought a girlfriend who stood about six-five. We called her Mrs. Short Dog. We asked Short Dog for some help with unloading the truck. Then I came across a butcher's knife.

"What's this?" I asked.

Johnny told me that our superior ordered the knife for Short Dog. Short Dog apparently asked for a better knife to do his chopping in the restaurant. I handed Short Dog the knife, and he stuck it down his pants.

"So, Short Dog, you like working here?" I asked the Dog.

"Yeah, it's alright."

"What did you do before this?"

"Time."

"What?"

"Time," he said more aggressively.

"What do you mean?"

"Locked up."

"You were in jail?" Johnny asked.

"Yeah. Damn straight."

"Why. What did you do?" I asked.

"There was this mother fucker. He wouldn't leave me alone. I was like, 'Just leave me alone, man.' But the motherfucker wouldn't leave me alone. He kept pushin,' man." Short Dog stopped there.

Johnny and I waited for the end of the story. Our outstretched necks attempted to lure the story out of Short

Dog's mouth like a king cobra and its enchanting charmer.

"So, what happened?" I asked.

"You killed him?" Johnny asked.

Short Dog shook his head. "Nah, I didn't kill 'im. I stuck 'im."

"You stuck him?" I asked.

"That's right."

"He stabbed him," Johnny informed me.

Johnny and I looked at each other, stunned.

"I said don't bug me, man," Short Dog stated and walked off into the concession stand to continue his cleaning.

Johnny and I began laughing.

"Well, I'm glad we just contributed to Short Dog's next slaying." Johnny said.

"Oh, brother. This place is jazzed up." Johnny and I laughed as we made our way upstairs to our office.

"Hey, Hakos," an eerie voice squeaked from behind, "Guitars gonna win, Hakos?" It was Buck Moss, two hours before game time. "Guitars gonna win?"

"No, Buck," I said.

"Why not?"

"Cuz they suck, Buck."

"No they don't."

"Whatever, Buck."

"You wanna touch the buckle?" Buck asked as he waddled his belly toward us.

"Make way!" We ran off for safety.

27 SOUTHERN HOSPITALITY

Not all was fun and games. I committed myself to a mission of finding a way to change the dangerous rubber hose that fed the propane to Hitler. I wanted something safer. I was sick of worrying that it might someday blow up. I figured I could find someone to either bury the hose or change the hose to a metal piping, something more durable. I decided to enlist the help of our propane man, the guy I sometimes called about finding additional pieces for the bastard Hitler. Moe was the man and grills and propane was his business, though he never really solved any of Hitler's problems. I called Moe and told him my dilemma. I left a message with the receptionist several times, but Moe never called back. I decided to take a trip to see Moe to ask his opinion. I loaded the celebrated truck with some propane containers and headed toward Moe's. Driving the highway in a truck with no doors was probably far from legal, but the breeze certainly felt cooling.

    I hopped out of the old truck and began, one-by-one, filling the propane tanks. After filling the propane, I entered the office and asked for Moe. After a long wait, Moe appeared. It looked as though he was going to walk right by so I shouted out, "Hey, Moe." He turned and looked at me blankly.

He answered slowly with his thick drawl, "Hey, you the guy from the Guitars."

"Yeah, hey, you know that rubber hose that leads from the big grill to the propane?" I asked this expecting an immediate nod of understanding, but Moe stared at me with such blankness that I could see the emptiness behind his eyes. He paused and answered, "No."

Confused, I tried again, "You know our big grill?"

"Yeah."

"Well the propane that's hooked up to that...you know that?"

"Yeah."

"There is a hose that connects them." I felt as though I was teaching a kindergarten class.

"Yeah."

"You know what I'm talking about?"

"Yeah."

I wasn't sure if Moe was the idiot or if I was. I continued, determined to explain my situation. I told him about the rubber hose and asked if he knew of a way to fix it. He thought and then began to speak with an unimaginable slowness, explaining to me that he originally linked the grill up to the propane by a hose because the ground underneath was all rock. There was no way to drill.

"So you can't put it underground?" I asked.

"No way." His Southern drawl increased with each word as if he was becoming some cartoon character.

"What about a metal link from the propane to the grill?" I asked, praying that I would spark some light in the man's brain.

"I don't do that kind of work." Moe spoke at a rate more leisurely than a grits-eating slug drowning in molasses.

I was getting impatient with the bastard so I asked, "Do you know anybody who does do this kind of work?"

He slightly paused and said in his expert drawl, "I haven't the slightest idea."

"You can't refer me to anyone?"

"Let me see." Moe walked off into the back halls of the office. Ten minutes passed. I turned to the receptionist and asked, "Is he coming back?"

"Who?" she replied. I walked out.

28 ADDED HILARITY

There we sat. It looked like the traditional bar setting. The television in the distance played ESPN. The older guys on the other side of the bar sat motionless. The coaster under my glass soaked up dribbled beer and condensation. Non-recognizable music drowned out the jokes my friends screamed in my ear. The smoke infiltrated the grooves of my corduroy jacket. The girl next to me swayed with drunkenness. The bartender took a constant order of beverages, usually taking three or four at a time. The gap between songs allowed for enough quiet to hear a few lines of my friend's joke.

Before long, the alcohol began taking its toll on the clarity of some of our heads. It was at this time that I noticed the girl next to me grinding on Todd's lap. I felt my face contort with confusion. What's going on here? Since when did these two become so close? And they were that close, her gyrating ass smothered Todd's groin. His jeans bunched up around his cock, and the girl's pants rode up close to her breasts due to the hard and constant grinding. My vision was a little blurred, so I leaned my head back, exercised my eyes, and turned back to Todd. The girl was indeed gyrating in Todd's crotch. The motion was so intense that she seemed to carve a groove out of his lap. I turned to Ricki and directed his attention to the sex-show being performed next to me. Together, we burst into snorted laugh. Just then, Todd turned to me.

"Hey, man, we gotta take this chick home."

"We do?"

"Yeah, shlee's too drunk to drive home," Todd answered, revealing a smidgen of drunkenness himself. "I'm gonna drive her home in her car. Do you mind following us?"

The relaxed bar-mood instantly disappeared with this idiotic question. All I wanted to do was to stay at the bar and chill out. Now, Todd was asking me to step out of my relaxation and enter into a state of responsibility. I wasn't up to it. A sudden depression set in, and I'm sure my face bunched with pain.

Todd noticed my lack of enthusiasm for his idea, "Is that'll right, man? If you don't want to that's cool."

I thought long and hard about the situation. I took a deep breath and answered, "Yeah, that's fine."

Next thing I knew, I was sitting in my idling car, searching for Todd and the gyrator. There! I spotted them a couple of rows away. Todd began to drive the girl's car through the parking lot. I crept my car behind a seemingly clueless Todd, who carelessly drove over the curb of the parking lot. As we exited the establishment, I noticed Peter pulling in. I rolled down my window to talk to him.

"Where are you going?" he asked.

"Todd's takin' this drunk chick home. I, like a dumbass, am following him. We'll be back." I shrugged my shoulders and Peter laughed and shook his head.

I turned my attention back to Todd and his new car. I pulled behind him at a stoplight. Then it hit me: Todd told me that the girl lived in Dixonville, which was a good 30 minutes away. Fuck. This was going to put a damper on the night. In addition to this driving catastrophe, I realized that I was in no shape to be driving, let alone Todd and his wobbling infatuation. I followed Todd down the interstate. His car swerved consistently from side to side. I thought that this was the end. I had this vision of a cop spotting

Todd's swerving. I quarreled with myself a lot—Damn! What are we doing? All I could think of was sitting comfortably at the bar. Shit. Here I am driving on a dark and barren road. The drive seemed to take forever. Where is this exit? It's gotta be coming soon.

Finally, we pulled onto an exit ramp. We took a right and a left and ended up turning into a driveway. The light on the garage made it difficult to see; however, I noticed Todd and his female companion exit the car and walk up to the house. Should I get out? Should I stay here? Fuck it. I'll see what's going on. I turned off my car and ran to catch up to the two drunken lovebirds. The girl knocked at the door, and the three of us waited there in drunken awkwardness.

The front door opened to reveal an older woman.

"Hi mom," our new friend said quite plainly.

"Mom?" I asked. We were assisting a drunken girl to her mom's house? Oh, fuck, how I wished to be sitting at the bar. My stomach sank with the sight of the mother. Mom looked us up and down with a peculiar investigative stare. Is it all right that we're here?, I questioned myself. I seriously doubted whether we were expected let alone invited. The girl introduced us to her mother with strict briefness. By this time, her younger sister also joined us at the door. She was probably no older than fourteen years old. I smiled with fright. Todd did the same. Our drunken gyrator squeezed passed her mother and sister. Todd and I quickly passed the awe-stricken family members and followed our drunken friend down a dark hallway. We turned into a room. Her bedroom? How old is this girl? The bedroom was decorated with stuffed animals and pink paint. Oh, fuck. What are we doing? I quivered to myself We are fucked. How old is this chick? Thoughts laced with fear raced through my head. Todd and I exchanged looks of discomfort. Just then, the mother yelled out for her drunken daughter. Our friend turned to us and said, "I just got a divorce. My mom's pissed at me. You guys stay here." My stomach repositioned itself above my intestines.

At least we weren't getting involved with a minor. I felt relieved knowing that she had been married. Thank God she's divorced, I thought.

"Where's the bathroom?" Todd asked. The girl took him by the hand and walked him out. There I stood alone in what looked like a teenybopper bedroom. I was hardly drunk anymore. The excitement of the night re-invigorated my senses. I noticed two figures walk by the door. I again felt uncomfortable. I looked around for something familiar; it was nowhere to be found. Instead, I merely snuck behind the bedroom door. Now I was safe.

As I stared at the back of the door, I heard stomping footsteps and whispered arguing whirl through the hallway. There was a definite fight ensuing between the mother and her drunken, divorced daughter. They seemed far away. For a moment, I thought I would make a dash for the door, but then I thought I should wait for Todd. I stood behind the door for what seemed like an hour.

There is not much to do while standing behind a door. I thought of better weekend nights—nights without thirty-minute, drunken drives to a divorcee's house. I thought of the time Ken, Peter, Brad, Todd and I ducked into the mock laser-gun game downtown. We paid for our guns and code names and strapped on our sensors and weapons. I decided to play the role of wartime reporter. I handed my gun to Ken and held tightly to my camera. The doors to the maze opened, and Ken took off running with me behind him in search of good footage to send home to the states. I hoped for a Pulitzer. Ken brilliantly fired both weapons with Billy the Kid perfection. I quickly followed, flashing my camera at fantastic shots that would disclose the truth of this laser battle. We bumped into Brad, and together, we managed our way through chaotic masses of bodies, strewn across the maze floor. The excitement awoke my athletic abilities of high school. We raced over barriers and dodged would-be assassins, all the while compiling a dazzling resume of photos. In the end, Ken and I ended up at the bottom of the ranks. We lost, but it beat out my time spent behind a divorcee's bedroom door.

My mind wandered toward a night when I ventured into the upstairs of a bar. The section was closed for the night, but I sneaked passed the bouncer whose spinning eyes moved from one big-bosomed girl to the next. I entered the dark bar on the second floor. No one was in sight. I crept behind the counter and crouched next to the taps. With my glass, I sat filling and refilling myself with good beer.

I also thought of a time when Ken and Todd dressed in these blow-up sumo suits the Guitars had for promotions in between innings. The two wore these inflated costumes downtown for Halloween. They definitely made a name for themselves. That had to have been better than this moment.

Long waits force people to look around as if something interesting might be found. For example, while waiting in the dentist's office, people slowly scan the room. What are they looking for? It's a fucking room with soiled magazines dated from the previous year—there is nothing to see. Well, I am as guilty of this as anybody, and I began scanning the room from behind the bedroom door. As you can imagine, my vision was dramatically reduced due to the fact that there was a door two inches from my face. About all I could do was scrunch my head to one side and examine the dresser that stood next to me. The top of the dresser sported a mess with random clutter. However, the dresser elevated a picture of our new drunken girlfriend and some boy. Is this her ex-husband? Did she keep this one picture to remind herself of him? Or, was it the guy she cheated on her ex-husband with? Or, was it just some dweeb from high school? I also caught sight of the articles of clothing in the top drawer...underwear! Why is everybody's top drawer filled with underwear? I stuck my finger in the drawer and began sifting through the different pairs of panties. There were blue ones and pink ones and even g-strings. Wow! What a variety. I quickly snatched a pair of blue panties that sat wrinkled on top, thought for a second, and grabbed the picture too. Souvenirs! I stuffed them both down my pants.

Just then, Todd entered. I viewed his every move from my limited position. He stopped by the side of the bed, looked around for a moment, and then sat on the bed. He looked miserable. His head turned from side to side. His eyes scanned his thoughts. I could tell that he was trying to figure a way out of this mess. Then, he began to talk to himself, "Fuck. Fuck it. Hakos. Where's Hakos? Where the fuck is Hakos? I gotta get outta here. Where's Hakos?"

All of this was quite entertaining, but I wanted to get the hell out of there too. I slowly revealed myself from behind the door. Todd looked up and disclosed no expression. We both knew what we had to do. Todd gave a nod, and I nodded back. He broke into a fast, robotic walk, and I followed. Our legs hurried us passed the drunkard's little sister like millipede legs when excited. We quickly continued our way down the hall and passed the mother. We made no eye contact; instead, we simply focused our heads in the direction of the front door. On our arrival to the front door, Todd swung the promised door open, we sped out, and I slammed it behind me. That ended our nonchalant approach to the departure. Once that door slammed shut, we both broke into a sprint for the car. I jumped in the driver seat, while Todd pounced on the passenger seat. I quickly threw the car into reverse, and, before I knew it, I was speeding down the street. We did all of this without talking. Finally, our silence broke.

"What the fuck was that?" I shouted.

"I don't know man," Todd answered. We both broke into a hysteric laughter. We knew the extent of the stupidity, and we knew that the mission had been a complete disaster. Nevertheless, the entire debacle created such a comic relief to the night that we had to praise our stupidity while we cursed it. Such idiocy was great in our minds.

We laughed and talked about the affair all the way back to the bar. When we made it back, we encountered all of our friends sitting there waiting for us. A unanimous "Where have you been?" sprung from their beer stained mouths. Without any answer, I pulled out the picture of the drunken girl and the boy, describing the mess we encountered by using the picture as an aide. I kept the panties stuffed deep in my pants.

29 THE BACHELOR AUCTION

It happened again. Early in the morning, before the rush, while enjoying the quiet and reading the front page of the newspaper, talk of sports destroyed my mood. It started as a tremor when a whoosh of air rushed through the front door. A couple of coworkers entered, barking sports crap back and forth, putting an end to my tranquility. My shoulders sank. My mind turned to the hours of hell ahead of me for that day. I picked myself up, the coworkers continued with their sports, and I slithered back to my concrete office.

When I ventured out again to get some envelopes from the main office, another conversation about sports streamed from the mouths of the employees.

They analyzed and assessed top players,
favorite players and even flop players.
They discussed players on streaks, at their peaks
or players whose socks rode high to their cheeks.
They diagramed defenses and devised detailed plays.
They rattled off records and praised playoff days.
They compared the third baseman of Pittsburgh of years ago
to the third basemen of the Red Socks and all his dough.
It tore at my ears until it forced tears.

Their talk pressed at my skull. The hairs on my head penetrated to my brain, causing sporadic quivers of annoyance to disrupt the regular workings of my organs. I sulked back to my office, wounded.

There I was, sitting at my desk. I was doodling on my calendar, avoiding people. I had given up my quest for grill safety. Instead, I was trying to get the drawing of one of the interns just right for my newest comic book, which starred several of the Mutant Interns (I was on book eight out of nine). Just as I was sketching his swirling hair, one of my coworkers walked in and presented me with the greatest of opportunities. It was the chance to leave Southtown with a bang.

"Hakos." Carson called.

"Yeah?"

"I got something for you I think you're really gonna like. If you don't like it, don't worry about it, just say no, but I think you're gonna like this one. When I heard about this, I thought I had to come straight to you."

"What is it?"

"Well, we did this thing with the Repertory Theater earlier in the season. And now the chick's coming back to me for a favor." Carson laughed a little. "They've got this bachelor auction thing going on, where they select guys from all over town, and they auction them off to these women. It's a way to raise money for the theater. They want some guys from the Guitars. This is going to be after the season, and I'm like, 'Well, the players won't even be here.' But she said she wanted anybody, just to raise money. Well, when I heard that, I'm like, 'I know just the guy.' So, do you want to?"

I looked around the concessions office at the other employees with a smile. With excitement, I screeched, "Yeah! Of course."

"I'm gonna see if I can get Todd to do it, and you guys can kind of go on as a double date." He paused for a second and added, "That was her idea."

"Even better. Hot dog!"

"So, you'll do it then?"

"Yeah, of course!"

"Well, I'm gonna set up a meeting between you guys, cuz she needs to interview you and get some information."

"Geez, this just keeps getting better."

Carson left me in a daydream. The earlier pain vanished. I saw myself walking out onto a gigantically long catwalk in the midst of colored lights and screaming women who would bid anything to have me. Then reality hit. I began to think of all other Guitars events—local chamber functions or little league outings, where people serve store-bought potato salad and some loud mouth southerner introduces the activities with inside jokes, while wearing a plaid shirt and jeans. Then I imagined the real picture: A picnic shelter with Todd and me standing in front of women wearing denim jackets with feathered hair and denim pants. We all kind of joke, and Todd and I say a few things about the Guitars. We get bought for ten or fifteen dollars, and then we take some picture for the organization's flyer. Finally, we jump in our car and drive two hours back home, ruining a perfectly good Saturday night. This was the vision I had, and I figured that it was pretty close to the truth. But who cared. This was a bachelor auction, and I couldn't think of anything sillier that I would more like to be a part of.

I walked over to the main office, and I looked for Todd. I couldn't find him, but I knew where he was. I walked down to the clubhouse where the weight room was. There was Todd pumping some iron.

"Hey," I tried to get his attention. The radio was playing loudly.

"Hey, Hakos."

"Hey, did Carson ask you about this bachelor auction thing?"

"No. What?"

Todd and I started taking turns bench pressing.

"Yeah," I started, "he just told me about this bachelor auction thing where he wants me and you to do it."

"What?"

"Yeah, I guess it's some big event for the Repertory Theater."

"Really?"

"Yeah."

"That sounds awesome."

"Do you want to do it? He said we could be like a double date."

"I don't know."

"Oh come on. It'd be great. Think of the story."

"You're right. That would make a great story. Alright."

"Yes!"

Together, Todd and I came up with a plan to perform some routine when we got up on stage, assuming there was a stage. We wanted to be wacky. We wanted to put on a show, and we were going to make sure that we were the best. We developed some stage moves in the weight room, taking turns strutting out onto the imaginary catwalk. Really dorky stuff.

We laughed and shook hands, solidifying our commitment. More pressing duties called, however. We went back to work, compiling minor league team addresses and inputting them into our spreadsheet—the spreadsheet of freedom—the key to our exodus from the Guitars.

Todd and I began printing off pages of resumes and cover letters. I collected about sixty team addresses and names of general managers to whom I was going to send resumes. Todd selected about one hundred. We made frequent visits to the mailroom for supplies. We were one step closer to working somewhere else, and the realization that the Guitars were history was becoming clearer.

We entered the final home stand, and the only energy in the air was produced from everyone's excitement that the season was coming to a close. For Todd and me, there was an added bonus; we were meeting with the lady from the bachelor auction.

We sat down with the lady in the Guitars advertising office. Todd wore his traditional pre-game gear, Guitars t-shirt and shorts. I wore a couple days' growth of stubble, shorts, my greasy rag that I carried wherever I went, a greasy t-shirt, and a neon orange jacket. The lady wore a black suit and skirt with high heels. Her face was serious, determined to get the job done. I immediately felt a clash of purpose between us.

First, she advised us to establish a prize that would accompany us to lure the women to bid on us. The auction lady suggested dinner, a limo ride, and a night at a Guitars game.

"That's pretty steep," I said.

"We would provide the dinner. We have donations from other organizations," she said.

"I have a client who has a limo service. I bet we could get them to do some trade," Todd suggested.

"Then, we would just need something else from you guys. Like a night in a sky box or something."

"Oh, yeah, that would be no problem. We could even make it 'Bring twenty of your friends,'" Todd proposed.

"Oh, you can do that?" she asked.

"Oh, yeah," Todd answered. I sat back and listened, while the two put together the details.

"Yeah, Todd's the salesman. I'm just the concession's guy. I could get ya some free hotdogs if you'd like?" I interjected jokingly. Todd laughed, and the lady half-smiled and looked back down at her list of questions.

"Now, I need to know some things about you guys," she said. She broadcasted some extra professionalism, which demanded compliance. She sat executive-like, cross-legged, while we more closely resembled the Mustard Man. Todd told her about himself. He was the Director of Sales. I was the Director of Concessions. Our occupations were not very alluring for horny southern belles. After getting our information, she told us where the event was being held and who might be there. The location was in one of the top notch hotels in downtown Southtown, a far cry from the hillbilly chamber functions I had imagined. To boot, Eddie George of the Tennessee Titans was going to be one of the bachelors. The lady left, and Todd and I could not stop laughing about the situation we had gotten ourselves into. We joked about the way we were dressed, and the fact that we were going to be bachelors in the same event as a professional football player. The event was going to be bigger than I had thought. The lady told us of the thousands of dollars that the event raised the previous year. This year they expected more. We also laughed at how the lady didn't laugh at any of my obnoxious jokes, like the one about having to buy a new wardrobe for the occasion. We thought that she was probably thinking, "Who are these bozos?" We were determined to be the best bozos.

During our last home stand, the concessions department broke the million-dollar mark. We celebrated in the office with a bottle of champagne. My superior celebrated for our broken record mark, but I celebrated the end of the season. We could do no wrong from here on out. After the final game, I had someone take my picture as I stood on the roof of the stadium with my back turned to the field. I crossed my arms in victory as the scoreboard glittered in the background. Afterwards, I walked down to Hitler to see how the Grillbillies were doing. The health inspectors never located the damn Hitler. The bastard sat there untouched, as if the dictator had found asylum in a bunker. I found the Billies in the cooler playing cards and drinking beer from a keg they took from one of the concession stand coolers. It was a beautiful sight—four Grillbillies crammed in a cooler, surrounded by cases of hotdogs and hamburgers. I slammed a beer with them and watched them compete in who could chug a bottled water the fastest. This event sickened me, and I left them to finish their games. I smiled.

After the season, the clean-up of the stadium was hard but fun. Todd and I received several offers from teams, and I knew for sure now that I was leaving the Guitars. Johnny and I did most of the concessions cleaning with the help of our old superior, but the mood was calmer, cleaner in a way.

With the end of the season came the end of the Guitars, or at least the Guitars that I knew. The Phantom brought in a new general manager. We had struggled the entire season without one, destroying any chance of organization, teamwork, or communication. Each department went its own way, making things all the more frustrating for me when I looked for help from the staff. Each time I called on the radio for help in unloading a delivery, I got little response. While packages came off the truck, I could see other employees walking the concourse, each claiming they had more pressing things at hand. With each department believing themselves to be more important, it made for a tense season. Attitudes rose and grudges formed. Many of the directors found little in common with the Phantom, who wanted to alter the operations of the team. Many employees agreed to contracts at the beginning of the season that failed to materialize. The Phantom found these contracts unacceptable. The new general manager came in with the job of firing anyone who disagreed with the Phantom. The Great Purge had begun.

The weekend before the Great Purge took place, I decided to leave the team. Although I hadn't accepted a job with another team yet, several teams seemed interested in me. I decided to walk in first thing on Monday morning and express my intention to leave. In the past, it would have been difficult for me to march into Al's office and tell him I was leaving. This wasn't Al. I felt no fear in walking straight into the general manager's office and shaking his hand good-bye. I walked up to the new general manager and told him that I was leaving. Later, I joined a team in Erie, Pennsylvania as their Director of Ticket Operations. When I arrived for the interview in Erie, I was going for the group sales position. I walked in to the interview, and the general manager asked, "So you're here for the Director of Tickets job?" whereupon I said, "Sure."

The new Guitars general manager told me to hold my thoughts on leaving. I had no idea that he planned to call every employee into his office for a meeting. Later that day, the Great Purge began. The new general manager called people into his office one-by-one and either fired or hired them. Most were fired. Todd was told that he didn't fit with the organization's plan. He was fired. Todd laughed. He didn't care, because a team in Tacoma hired him, and he didn't start work for a couple of months, allowing him to plan a backpacking trip to Europe. When I walked in, the new general manager said, "So, you've expressed your wishes to leave."

"I am leaving," I corrected the man.

"Well, we were hoping to keep you. I heard good things about you."

"I appreciate that, but I've done my time here, and I'm leaving."

"Well, it's too bad I didn't get to know you."

"Yes it is, and I wish you luck here." I shook the man's hand and walked out. I couldn't hide the grin that took over my face. I waved bye to all who were watching me walk out of the new guy's office. I strolled back to the concessions office and packed up my junk. I was no longer a Southtown Guitar. The relief was amazing. All my bad moods and anger left. I was a free man, and for a few weeks, I had no job to drive to in the morning. I stood for a moment in the concessions office. I meditated for a moment, attempting to find some pain in me. None. I was cleansed. I couldn't even try to fire myself up about some irritating problem. My liberation ignited the positive being in me.

The loss of a job didn't sit well with everyone. About thirteen of the twenty-one office workers were canned. Relations had become so heated during the season that the purging heightened problems for the ownership.

The local media and residents took offense. Before the Al years, the Guitars lost much of its fan base. The previous ownership allowed Guitars games to dwindle into

Sweaty Mascots start Grease Fires

a boring outing. Al created an environment of enthusiasm that brought the people of Southtown back to the stadium. This energized people, and the attendance skyrocketed as the employees worked hard to rebuild the Guitars.

Shocked upon hearing of the firings, the local sports talk radio guys couldn't help but discuss the upheaval in the Guitars office. They focused on the firing of the Guitars number one announcer, who they thought should be a professional announcer. They talked about the whole episode like it was a travesty. The two radio personalities talked about it for a while before opening the line up for callers.

They asked, "Does this bother some of you?"

The first caller was a lady who praised the released staff and complained about the fact that the new general manager had no baseball experience. The hosts agreed with the caller, and they continued blasting the firings on their own, "This looks like 'One Flew Over the Cuckoo's Nest.'" They implored the ownership to straighten itself out before things got any worse. They took the next caller.

"Let's go to Brad in Southtown."

"I don't think it's about salary per say. It's about the owner wanting to put in his own regime." It was Grillbilly Brad!

One of the radio guys asked Brad why the owner would keep one announcer and not the other.

"To my understanding, the other guy had more experience on the business end and could work during the off-season." Brad began revealing the true happenings to all of Southtown.

The radio guys were still confused, "How much of a dumbbell do you have to be after the success the Guitars have had in the last two years?" They agreed with Brad's opinions.

Then Brad opened the door all the way, "The new general manager is being influenced by (the Phantom)."

There was a silence on the radio. Then, one of the radio guys said, "I'd like to keep you on the air here Brad, cuz it sounds like you know something. Is that true?"

"Yeah. I was fired."

"You were one of the ones fired?" A more solemn tone came over the radio guys.

"Yeah."

"Can you get fairly specific with us, Brad?"

Brad dove into an explanation, disclosing information about the Phantom and the owner. He gave examples of the Phantom's fingerprints and how the team was changing.

"What reason did he give you for being fired? Was it lack of performance?"

Brad quickly answered, "I can guarantee it wasn't lack of performance. But I'm not sure what it was. He just told me that I didn't fit into his plans."

"What were those plans?"

"I don't know. He didn't tell me."

"Brad let me ask you this, and then we'll let you go, cuz we had no idea someone involved in this was gonna call. Are there more firings to come?"

"Yeah. Couple more... two or three."

It was clear that the guys on the radio didn't want this call to end. They had found the jackpot. They repeated a couple times that they would let Brad go, but they kept asking questions.

"Let me say one more thing. I do want to say that I am sorry for what happened to you. For the eleven of you who were canned, thank you for your work the last two years. You have saved baseball in this city, cuz it was dadgumneardead (this is as close of an interpretation as I can make of what this guy said) before you guys came in and saved it."

"Thanks. It's nice to know someone appreciated it more than the owner and (the Phantom)." Brad hung up, leaving the lines open for a string of disappointed callers.

Sweaty Mascots start Grease Fires

I listened to the radio broadcast with Todd. We sat back in our chairs, unable to clear the grins from our faces. It was true that it was nice to hear someone appreciate our work. I hadn't heard many "thanks" in the past couple of years, but this one "thank you" made up for all the unsaid ones. I knew the complications in the office during the season upset Brad and I made sure to praise him for calling in on our behalf. Even though I left on my own accord, I was part of the team, and the purges affected us all.

That was the end of the Guitars. I enjoyed leaving the team with some controversy. I didn't want the whole thing to end quietly; I had put too much of my time into the Guitars to have it fade into the background. Unfortunately, this wasn't the end for many of us. The purging got ugly, as contracts with former employees were broken. Lawsuits were filed and a year of court battling ensued.

After the purges, Todd and I celebrated at home by cracking open a beer. The Heineken still sat on the balcony, but it was hardly good anymore. We used it as more of a breeding ground for unknown insects. With our beers, we began practicing moves for the bachelor auction. Todd decided to bring his yo-yo on stage, and after walking to the front of the catwalk, Todd planned to sling his yo-yo. I thought it was a terrific idea. I needed a catchy move. I decided to bring a cigarette and light it up on stage—that would get the ladies. We also decided to walk out together at some point and whip our jackets off together. This demanded an appropriate shirt underneath the jacket. Since we had been working out, we decided to be extremely garish and wear tight revealing shirts. We agreed to go shopping for a good tough-guy shirt. We walked out to our balcony and drank a couple more beers. We came up with the plan to have someone film the event. It needed to be documented, we thought, and we knew Ken would do it. We called Ken up and talked him in to following us around for the night with the movie camera.

That evening, the phone rang. I was in my room, playing guitar with the door wide open—I felt no need to lock myself away anymore. I answered the phone.

"Hakos?"

"Al?"

"Yeah." It was Al. He was calling for Todd, but I talked with him for a bit.

"How are you?" I asked.

"Fine. I'm in Beloit right now with a team up here."

"Oh, great."

"Yeah. It's going pretty well. We don't quite have the guys that we had down there, but it's going well."

"Cool."

"What are you up to? No more Guitars, huh?"

"Nah, fuck that," Al laughed, and I was surprised that I possessed the confidence to talk to Al in that manner. "I got a job in Erie."

"Closer to home, huh."

"Yeah, about a good cigar's smoke away."

"Oh, yeah?"

"Yeah." It was great talking to Al. I felt a real growth with the way I carried myself. Sure, it was a short phone call, but I didn't stumble or stutter through the conversation. I talked to Al as if we were equals. I grabbed Todd and gave him the phone. I sat back in my room, proud.

The night of the bachelor auction arrived. I showed Ken how to work my camera and we headed downtown to the hotel. Todd and I wore sport coats with tight t-shirts underneath. Todd also sported an Oregon Ducks baseball cap. When we walked into the hotel, an unknown woman dressed in a very beautiful evening gown said, "Oh, you're the Guitars guys. Your dates get sky boxes and a limo ride."

"Yeah," I answered baffled, "how did you know?"

"I recognize you from the pictures."

"Really?" I was surprised. We introduced ourselves, and introduced Ken as the photographer.

She showed us the program booklet, which pictured all the bachelors and gave a little biography of each. We noticed by far that we had the smallest income out of any of the bachelors. There were doctors, lawyers, writers, singers, and sports players. She pointed out a puppy that was resting on a table.

"The ladies can bid on the dog if they don't find any suitors among the men," she said. A fitting trade, some might say.

The woman also showed us the ballroom where everything was to be held. It was enormous and superbly decorated. There was a huge catwalk surrounded by a hundred tables. It was darkly lit, and it boasted the Southtown skyline as its backdrop. My stomach dropped in awe. I shook off my intimidation with a gulp and turned to Todd and stated, "This is going to make a great story."

We had some time to spare so we made our way to the hotel bar, where we sat in the corner preparing ourselves.

"This thing is huge," I said.

"No shit. This is amazing," Todd replied.

"Did you guys know it was going to be this big?" Ken asked.

"No clue," we said in unison.

Todd brought a flask filled with Jack Daniels. We all took a swig before ordering more drinks. The waitress brought us our drinks, and we ordered the next round right then. This event needed some artificial inspiration. Ken turned on the camera and proceeded to interview us at our table.

"What kind of girl are you looking for, Hakos?" he asked.

"Well, I'm not really here to find a girlfriend, so I don't really want any young chick slobbering all over me. I would rather have some rich old lady bid on me. I think I would feel more comfortable that way. Plus, I might be able to swim at her big pool, naked."

"What about you, Todd?"

"You know what I want? I just want somebody fun. Cuz you know what? Fun is fun."

After about twenty minutes of drinking at the bar area, we decided to venture into the party. The whole event took up several rooms. Two rooms contained food and drinks. Currently, it was the mingling hour, and we were supposed to be increasing our bids by sweet-talking the ladies. All around the room, women in extravagant evening gowns graced the floor, surrounded by fashionably catered food. Some women were old and some were young.

I allowed my awe to walk me through the rooms and from table to table. I picked up drink after drink from bars squeezed in every corner.

We bumped into a psychiatrist who was another bachelor. His confidence radiated heavily from his loud mouth. He was so wrapped so tightly into himself that his round belly was firm like a basketball. Funny thing, he was wearing almost the identical outfit as Todd and me. He acted like the professional bachelor, coaching us on how to work the room. He told us all about the event.

"Now, do you guys have a shtick?" he asked.

"Yeah." We looked at each other laughing.

He almost seemed disappointed and added, "No, like a real gimmick. Like this is what I got. I'm takin' my girl to Marti Gras, so I'm gonna bring out some beads and throw them into the crowd, like at actual women." Todd and I acted surprised, "Now, the lights out there are blinding. The lights will be staring ya right in the face. So you just pretend to see the ladies. You know, point and all that. That way they think you really want them. Then, toss the beads. I have extra. Do you want some?"

"Nah, we got our own thing. But thanks," I said.

A few girls walked up, and the psychiatrist took over the show. She asked us, "Who are you guys?"

I was about to talk when Mr. Psycho talked right over me, "Let me show ya. He looked out into space and raised his arm as if he was some lounge singer. Then he proceeded to use his quote from the printed program,

"Party girl, get your craziest costume, cuz you're goin' to Marti Gras."

"Oh, you're the psychiatrist!" the lady exclaimed.

"Yeah." I will never forget his face when he said this. It was such a stupid, smiley, cartoonish, goofy face that I almost puked out my soul because I wanted no longer to be a part of a soul that witnessed this moment; instead I coughed out a laugh.

I slinked away from Mr. Psycho, but I made sure to mark him down as someone to revisit. The guy was like a bad television show that keeps pulling you back for more. Ken drifted off into the crowd and started interviewing unknown people. Todd and I got cornered by a group of older women. These women were a definite product of old Southern money, and they possessed a sophistication that rose well beyond our level. They asked us questions about what we did. Usually, Todd provided the facts, while I interjected corny one-liners. I took this opportunity to scan the room. I saw Ken interviewing the chef about the roast beef and I saw a guy wearing a polo uniform, but no Eddie George. Eddie was playing my Cleveland Browns the following week, and I was trying to think of some way I could screw up his play. Maybe I could make him drink a lot so he would get alcohol poisoning and be out for a week. Maybe I could persuade a girl to bid on him and chain him in a hotel for a week. I wasn't sure what I could do, but the old ladies' talk was boring enough that I could mastermind quite a few evil plans.

We tore away from the wealthy broads and found some younger girls. These girls hoped to pull their purses together in order to purchase a bachelor. Todd and I worked this table quite a bit, and Ken made sure to document it. He asked them all to introduce themselves to the camera, making sure to zoom in on their breasts. I got talking to a blonde who was pretty good looking. I told her about myself, and she told me that she wanted the dog that was sitting in the next room. I liked that about her so I asked her if she wanted to find Eddie George with me. We walked off into the crowd. Todd stayed behind and wooed the rest of the table, while Ken continued his interviewing.

Ken tried to get as many girls as he could to say, "Good luck Todd and Hakos!" He was doing quite well. Many groups thought that Ken was either working for the theater or filming a documentary. A few of the people he talked to asked him questions about the event. Some girls asked Ken if he was going to be auctioned off. In fact, I think Ken found more possible dates than Todd or me.

One girl asked Ken, "So how is this going to work? Are they going to ask these guys questions? Is it going to be like the Miss America pageant, where they'll have to say how they're going to save the world or the children?"

I still hadn't found Eddie George, but when I bumped into Ken, he told me that he filmed George. That satisfied me but not the blonde I was with. Just then, someone walked around the room asking people to take their seats for the show. The blonde told me that she would find me later, and she joined her group. Then, a group of ladies approached me and told me they had been waiting to talk to me all night.

"Really?" I was quite surprised.

"You're the..." she motioned with her arms like she was hitting a hockey puck, "...the hockey guy."

"Yeah," I went along with it.

"You look a lot shorter without your gear on."

"Yeah, well that's a lot of gear. You know, the helmet."

"Yeah, so you're going to be auctioned?" Asking all the questions was an attractive red head. She was surrounded by a group of women.

"Yes. Of course. That's why I'm here."

I found out that she was a doctor, and the ladies with her were nurses. She eventually found out that I was with the Guitars when Todd came over and was unaware of the massive fibbing that was taking place. In defense of myself, I said, "Hey, whatever it takes to get you ladies to bid on me." The doctor told me about a pool party she was having at her house in the hills. I asked her how I could get on the guest list, and she told me that she could arrange it. Then, they walked into the ballroom to seat themselves.

Ken ran up to a lady and asked if she would root for us, and the lady responded, "Haven't we done this before?"

"Let's do it again," Ken insisted.

Then Ken turned to Todd and asked him if he had any last words. Todd replied, "How did Custer feel before the Alamo?" Todd's confidence was fading, along with his historical accuracy.

I ran to the restroom, and Todd found a secure spot in the back of the room. We weren't to go on stage until the end, so we had plenty of time to wait and drink. One of the members of the Repertory Theater who was running the event approached Todd and asked if he wanted a drink. She was an attractive girl. Todd took advantage of this and accepted the drink offer. I returned from the bathroom to see that Todd had hit the jackpot. I began talking to another of the Repertory Girls in the back. She was a tall redhead, and she was, in my opinion, the most attractive girl there, and she was married. I took comfort knowing she was married—no stress. I liked talking to her because she was cute and she laughed at my stupid jokes—perfect woman.

As Todd and I worked it in the back of the ballroom, Ken found a seat with another group of girls just to the side of the catwalk. An announcer came on stage and introduced the event. He told the crowd that the money raised was going to fund the Repertory Theater. Each woman in the crowd was armed with a paddle to bid with, and an auctioneer walked on stage to do her fast-talking auction voice. The bidding began at one hundred dollars as Eddie George thundered onto the stage. They asked George about his ideal date, and then the music blasted in as George walked the catwalk. He was very stiff and uncomfortable, probably cursing his agent in his head.

The auctioneer started, "Do I hear one hundred? One hundred dollars. One hundred dollars there. One fifty..." the bidding continued all the way to $9,250. Finally, Eddie walked off the stage, and the lucky girl walked up and hugged him. They walked out into the lobby together, and I followed. I still didn't know how I was going to foil the leg strength of Eddie George. I approached the all-pro and asked, "Eddie, would you mind going easy on my Browns next week?"

He stopped and smiled somewhat uncomfortably and answered, "I could possibly do that." (I would find the following week that Eddie possibly did nothing but run all over my Browns.)

The bachelors came and went. The music continued to boom with the sounds of hip-hop. Screaming women cheered and sighed, but none of the bachelors did anything special. I knew that Todd and I were going to show this crowd what cat walking at a bachelor auction was all about.

Girls brought us more drinks, and then they escorted us back stage, where there was a table full of bottles of alcohol.

"We should have just come back here at the beginning," I said.

We bumped into Mr. Psycho again, swinging his beads. He was going on before us, and he began prepping us on what needed to be done.

"Are you nervous?" he asked.

I wanted to tell him, "No, I'm drunk." Instead, I just said, "No, I feel pretty good."

Todd still hit on his girl who had followed us back stage. Then the lady who interviewed us approached. She was the lead organizer of the event, and she drilled us with the specifics of the stage. While she was talking to us, I picked up a bottle of Jack and took a couple of swigs.

"Hey, don't do that," she said with a feeling motherly disapproval. I just raised my eyebrows in innocence. She threw her hand up and said, "Oh, go ahead." I took the bottle.

We were each going to have an escort take us on stage. We were going to be asked questions, and then we had to walk the catwalk.

"Together?" Todd asked.

"Whatever you want?" she said.

Todd turned to me, "What should we do?"

"We'll do the plan, and then go from there," I responded.

While we talked to the lead organizer, Mr. Psycho walked out on stage to do his shtick. He walked out to the front of the catwalk, where he removed his jacket to reveal a firmly round belly. Then, he pulled his beads from his jacket, and tossed them into the crowd. All the while, he smiled and made imaginary eye contact with people he couldn't see. He pointed out into the blackness, as if he saw a girl screaming for beads. Then, after spotting his imaginary girl, he expressed a surprised look on his face and smiled. Finally, he tossed a set of beads. It was great buffoonery. On film, it looks surprisingly good.

Finally, it was our turn. Two girls took us by the arms and escorted us to the stage. First, the announcer introduced us. We were measly employees of a minor league baseball club (well, we were a couple of days prior). The announcer described our date, and he asked Todd, "Twenty of her friends get to go into a sky box?"

Whereupon, Todd answered with a shrug, "Sure." We were no longer employed by the Guitars, but we were handing out a certificate for a night in a skybox.

Then the announcer asked us about ourselves. When he approached me, he asked me how I felt below the belt. I answered, "Loose." The room filled with drunken women cried out in pleasure.

He followed that question with another, "What are you looking for in a woman?"

"Someone who can maximize the looseness," I answered.

"Maximize the looseness. Alright," he bellowed with fantastic announcer-like corniness.

The music charged in, and Todd and I began our strut on the catwalk.

At first we modeled our way to the edge and walked back. Then, Todd swaggered out by himself. When he got to the end, he whipped out his yo-yo and gave it a whirl. The women erupted into a wild craze. When I heard the reaction, I knew we had them. They were in for a show. My turn arrived. I walked out by myself, still unsure of what to do, but when I got there I broke into a wild tap dance with flailing arms. Again, the crowd erupted. I walked back with a powerfully arrogant strut. Todd and I looked at each other and agreed it was time to take the jackets off. We were addicted to the attention. We had no idea that anybody was bidding on us. In fact, we had no idea where we were, but we did know that whenever we walked out on the catwalk there exploded a grand cheer from hundreds of women. We walked out together; I lit a cigarette on the way out, took a puff, and flung it into the crowd. Todd and I looked at each other and threw our jackets off, revealing our tough guy shirts. Todd's eyes opened wide as he flexed for the crowd. I stood there sporting the presence of Hercules. I walked back, but Todd didn't follow. Instead, he struck a body-builder pose and showed his muscles to the crowd. The boy was possessed. He began to gyrate his pelvis around, forcing the crowd to stand and scream. Finally, Todd walked back. For the first time, I could hear the bidding. It was up to $700. We needed more. The auctioneer turned to me and said that the crowd wanted more. She said that they wanted to see a trick or something. As soon as she said trick, the idea hit me. I swaggered down the runway and pulled out my handkerchief. When I got to the end, I showed the crowd the handkerchief. I began stuffing it into my hand as if I was doing a magic trick. When I had stuffed the entire thing into my hand, I showed my stuffed fist to the crowd and then quickly threw the handkerchief behind me. I held up my hands to reveal nothing. Of course, the whole trick was a blatant bust, but the girls screamed even louder. How was that for a trick? I began to walk back, and on my way back, I passed Todd who confidently marched back out and whose face expressed a determined glow. He got to the end of the walkway and began taking his shirt off. He had lost it. He took his shirt and swirled it into the crowd. He danced a little dance and walked back. When all was final, we went for $725. Our added antics only increased our worth by twenty-five dollars.

We met the lucky winners. They were friends of the girls who worked for the Repertory Theater. We all got together and talked for a while, and then we told the girls that we would call them with a good time to go out for dinner and a limo ride. We gave them the free pass for the skybox and bid farewell.

Before we left, Todd and Ken got numbers from a couple girls. Then we had a nightcap with the doctor and her nurses in the bar. I never did get an invitation to that pool party.

A few nights later, the three of us watched the video with Peter. Todd and I had called the girls the day before to see if they could go on the date in the next couple of days, but they said that they were busy. We were leaving the state in the next couple of days, and we knew that the dates would never happen.

30 DEPARTING, THE HAKOS PARTY

Todd, Ken, and I indulged in a final Southtown dinner. The next day I was leaving for Erie, and Todd was leaving for Europe. Earlier in the day, I packed a U-haul full of my belongings. Todd and I threw the unwanted furniture and junk into a dumpster. We checked out of the apartment, and we stayed in a Holiday Inn for the night. (During the season I received a free room with the hotel when I made a trade with them for some tickets.) It was a quiet night. We said bye to Ken and retired to our free room. I told Todd that I was getting up around 4 a.m. He thought that was ludicrous, and thought it best if we said our good-byes before we went to bed. We knew we would meet up again even though we were moving to opposite ends of the country, so the parting was not too dramatic.

    When 4 a.m. rolled around, I jumped out of bed, and Todd didn't even move. I threw on some clothes and boarded my U-haul. I felt comfortable in a truck nowadays, considering the experience I gained from trucks at the stadium. I waved goodbye to the Holiday Inn dumpster that was filled with our couch, one of our chairs, and a whole lot of useless junk. I jumped onto the interstate and followed it north. I saluted the lit Southtown skyline and continued on my way. I left a changed man. I was no longer the bright-eyed, naïve boy who originally came, and I was no longer the man who was going to be stifled by anger either. Instead, I was a man who knew he could change when he wanted to, in order to be happier—whether that was a change of job or a more immediate change of mind. Though I was hardly perfect, I felt that I possessed a greater control of my life. I had taken an active role in deciding my future. I knew what I was doing.

When 5 a.m. rolled around, I decided to light a cigar. I was having trouble lighting the bastard and my truck swerved into the other lane. Before I knew it, a police cruiser trailed me with its lights flashing. I pulled over. The officer walked up alongside the truck to the window.

"Boy," the officer said in a wonderfully thick Southern tongue, "how long you been drivin'?"

I smiled and told him about my cigar. He told me to be careful in such a large machine. He looked inquisitively at the passenger seat. There, next to me, sat a pair of blue panties—something I found as I moved out of my room. He looked back at me. I smiled and he let me go, and I continued on my way up Interstate 65, exiting the state of Tennessee soon after. I thought being stopped by the cop was an appropriate way to leave my stay in beautiful Southtown. It seemed almost symbolic of my life in the South. I had been stopped momentarily and tested but, in the end, I escaped a happy man.

ABOUT THE AUTHOR

Anton Hakos lives in Akron, Ohio with his wife, two cats, and dog. Now a vegan, Hakos still takes pride in being a grillbilly and can cook a mean veggie burger.

Hakos is happy to finish his first book and looks forward to future publications. He also writes poetry and fiction. .

DISCUSSION QUESTIONS

1. In the book, Hakos finds himself in a job that is frustrating and depressing him. What was your worst job? What did you learn from that job?

2. Hakos begins the story as a naïve college graduate and learns a lot from this job. What life experiences does he learn, and have you had a similar "teacher"?

3. Did you ever want to be fired from a job?

4. Al judges Hakos because of the car he drove. Do people get an inaccurate impression of you because of your car, clothes, the way you talk, etc?

5. The Grillbillies drop hotdogs on the ground and cook questionable chicken because they were scared of not coming through with the food. Hakos finds himself dismissing ethics in favor of getting the job done. Discuss.

6. Hakos struggles to sell something he doesn't believe in. Could you sell baseball? Is there something you could sell? Couldn't sell?

7. Hakos gains confidence when he wears the Fuzzy costume to the shareholders party. If you could change your identity for a day, who would you be?

8. Why does the Phantom want to keep Hakos on the staff? Was it right for him to quit or should he have stayed and used his experience to his advantage to help rebuild the team?

9. Hakos gives in to peer pressure throughout the book. Do you find it disturbing that he often finds himself in x-rated, irresponsible situations?

10. How much would you pay for Hakos and Todd at the bachelor auction?

Made in the USA
Charleston, SC
09 June 2011